ExploraCenter

A Hands-on
Classroom Science Museum

Grade 4 Activity Booklet

By

Joseph Abruscato
University of Vermont

Paul Doherty
Center for Teaching and Learning
at the Exploratorium

Ed Rock
ScottForesman

ScottForesman Science

Discover the Wonder

Design by Amy O'Brien Krupp.
Illustration for activity cards by B.J. Johnson.
Illustration for pages iii, iv, 1, 2, 3, 4, 65, 75, 76, and 80 by Douglas Klauba.
Explorabook text by Anne Hayes and the Exploratorium staff.
Explorabook illustrations by Elwood Smith.
Science and educational review by Paul Doherty, Cappy Greene, and the Exploratorium staff.

ISBN 0-673-42844-3

2 3 4 5 6 7 8 MH 99 98 97 96 95 94 93

ScottForesman

A Division of HarperCollins*Publishers*

Contents

Preface

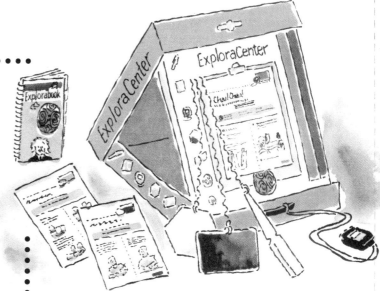

Welcome to the ExploraCenter, a free-standing science center designed to support Scott-Foresman's *Discover the Wonder* science series. The ExploraCenter offers you and your students a place to initiate all kinds of marvelous inquiries into the wonders of science. But, above all, it creates for students a place to go and do science.

The ExploraCenter is like a children's science museum—right in your classroom. It is designed to excite, stimulate, and channel students' innate curiosity about science. It will visually and intellectually draw students in—almost as if it were a black hole for curious minds, drawing students in through a strong, seemingly mysterious force.

Tools

Six science tools come with the center:

magnet

stopwatch

diffraction grating

magnifying (or Fresnel) lens

reflective paper

thermal card

In the pages that follow, you will find an introduction to each tool, along with one introductory activity using the tool. Play around with the tools. Try them out. Encourage students to do the same. Then try one of the "starter" activities. Each of the other activities gives students experiences related to the modules in *Discover the Wonder*—about five opportunities in each module to do hands-on science.

Purpose

You may use the ExploraCenter in a variety of ways, depending upon what best fits your classroom and teaching style. It works as a: 1) formal, hands-on extension to the modules in the *Discover the Wonder* program, 2) permanent science exhibit for your class where students can perform experiments and demonstrate scientific understanding, and 3) sort of "scientific jungle gym" where students are free to explore and let their curiosity run wild.

Explorabook by Klutz

The ExploraCenter also includes *Explorabook,* the best-selling science book by Klutz Press. It can become for you a portable extension of the ExploraCenter, because both are so similiar in approach and spirit. (After all, John Cassidy and Klutz Press were gracious enough to co-develop the ExploraCenter with ScottForesman expressly for teachers.) Use the *Explorabook* to extend hands-on learning about science. Leave it lying around the classroom. A teacher's guide for it, written by Anne Hayes of the Exploratorium in San Francisco, appears on pages 66–75.

What Is the ExploraCenter?

What about a short tour of the ExploraCenter? First, take a look at the outside, which we affectionately call "the pizza box." Notice that we have designed the box so that it will invite students to look it over on all sides, to read it, explore it, and eventually, open it. (Plus, it folds up so you can store it conveniently.)

Now open the box, lifting up on the side with the handle. Pull up the inner flap (the ExploraCenter board). The top of the board has a ledge, which, when you pull the board all the way forward, will attach to the inside of the top of the box. This ledge locks into position to create an easel for displaying activities and recording science observations and data.

Note that the board has a shiny surface, which students can write on and then wipe clean with a wet tissue. Caution students to use a washable crayon or a similar type of wipe-off marker.

You have obviously already found this teacher's guide inside the ExploraCenter box.

Did you also find the tools? The ExploraCenter tools are:

- Fresnel lens
- reflective paper
- diffraction grating
- stopwatch
- magnet
- thermal card

Follow the instructions on the inside of the top of the box so that you can attach the tools to the board using the leashes provided. Also, above the words "Activity Card" you can attach the blackline masters from this activity guide.

Once you've attached the tools, you and your students are ready to begin. Almost everything you will need is already in the ExploraCenter (some very accessible and low-cost items are needed to supplement some of the activities). A comprehensive list of additional materials needed for the activities is given on page 80 of this guide.

Now, let's move to the activity cards themselves, which you can easily attach to the board. The activities are free-standing. They do not depend on each other, and they can be done in any order you choose. Each activity is accompanied by a teacher's page that lets you know any necessary background for the activity and what to expect as the activity's outcome, as well as some extensions and additional challenges.

That completes the tour. We hope you will enjoy and use the ExploraCenter for years to come.

How the ExploraCenter Works

The ExploraCenter works all by itself. Just set it up and watch kids play with it. To appreciate science and learn about it, children need to participate. That's what the ExploraCenter does: it provides a place and a way to do science.

The activities provided in the ExploraCenter will systematically expose students to the science concepts found in *Discover the Wonder.* These activities 1) direct students to experience a concept or phenomena personally, then 2) challenge them to extend the experience, 3) suggest research that can be done to enhance their understanding, and 4) call for action to be taken related to the experience.

These activities can be done by a single student, but, if you encourage small groups of students to tackle an activity cooperatively, your classroom will more accurately mimic a real science laboratory, and your students' behavior and interaction will more accurately reflect a real scientific endeavor.

Invitation to Learn

Each activity begins with a unique and thought-provoking question that challenges and encourages the student to discover. In other words, the student is invited to learn. Of course, this invitation also serves to focus and motivate students. He or she will enter the activity with an open and curious mind and a willingness to seek answers.

Opportunities to Explore

Through a series of basic instructions, students explore the concept or phenomena. They are asked to make a variety of observations or, to put

it more simply, to experiment with the stuff. This part of the activity provides the student with valuable experiences because this initial exposure can lead to additional "what ifs."

Encouragement to Explain

After an initial set of experiences with the phenomena or concept, students will typically seek out the "answer" from a resource. Students can also pursue their own answers through discussion with other students.

Call to Take Action

There is a call to action, asking students to solve a problem posed or create a device that will accomplish some task. This action allows students to internalize the information they have related to the concept or phenomena and do something real about it.

Open-Ended Inquiry

While all of the activities have some direction to get students started, students always have the opportunity to branch off on their own paths of inquiry.

Why Open-Ended Inquiry Is Important

The ExploraCenter provides 30 activities (5 or more for each module in the *Discover the Wonder* program), which includes a series of introductory activities to get students started. The purpose of the ExploraCenter and its activities is to involve students in open-ended, hands-on activities.

The value of the open-ended activities is that they allow students to take the conceptual knowledge they have acquired and make use of it in a controlled, applied way. The number of solutions to the challenges will be limited only by students' creativity.

When students complete the "What to do" section of each activity, they are gathering background information and experiences. From that starting point, they are challenged to solve a problem or accomplish a related task.

The activities also provide a challenge to stimulate open-ended inquiry. This challenge, called "Can you . . .," is the final element on the student activity pages for grades 3-6. This opportunity for open-ended inquiry caps off the experience at the ExploraCenter by allowing the students to solve a problem using all the conceptual and process development skills they have accumulated during a *Discover the Wonder* module.

In the teacher's notes, we have provided some direction and a suggestion for a possible solution to the challenge. However, while students are working on the challenge, it is important to remember a few general guidelines.

1. Any workable solution that students develop is valid.
2. It is OK for students to struggle with solutions to the challenges. They are learning that persistence and creativity pay off.
3. It is OK for them to enlist the aid of peers. They are learning that collaboration is the rule rather than the exception in the scientific community.
4. It is OK for them to ask you what the solution might be. They are learning that a good scientist must utilize all the available resources.
5. Do not suggest a solution too soon. Students should see that every problem, no matter how difficult it may seem, may not have a solution that is immediately within reach. The struggle and the testing of many hypotheses are critical to the development of a self-sufficient problem-solver.

Overall, try to be a reference, a sounding board, or a consultant to your students. Resist the urge to give a solution, but never resist the opportunity to offer support and encouragement.

How to Use the ExploraCenter for Assessment

We have intentionally omitted student recording sheets and worksheets from the ExploraCenter. Students are encouraged to just do the science! Data collection and comparison are handled at the ExploraCenter's board. Keeping in mind that a full and formal set of assessment options are available in the *Discover the Wonder* science program, you can also accomplish informal assessment at the ExploraCenter:

1. Students' participation at the ExploraCenter should be viewed as positive, and students should be given some small extra credit for simply participating in an activity.

2. Careful observation of students and their interaction with the ExploraCenter activity will provide you with a feel for the level of proficiency that each student has in manipulating science materials.

3. Observation of students doing an activity at the ExploraCenter, and their interaction with peers, will provide information on the ability of each student to interact effectively with others.

4. Also, by noting students who are successfully able to complete the Challenge portion of the

activity, you can award extra credit and evaluate each student's determination and, to a degree, creativity and problem-solving ability.

5. Finally, you can easily note which science processes are dominant in the ExploraCenter activity (they are noted on your ExploraCenter teacher pages). Observe students as they perform the activity. Note the ease or difficulty each student experiences as he or she moves through the activity (0=Can't do the activity at all; 1=Tried to do the activity but was unable to complete the task; 2=Was able to complete the activity).

You will be able to identify each student's mastery of that science process. If you make an observational measurement of students at the beginning of the year, and then observe the students at the end of the year doing an activity emphasizing similar process skills, you will be able to note development of process-skill ability.

The ExploraCenter is a place for children to go and have fun doing science. You may also want to provide credit or otherwise positively reward children simply for participating in these and any other science activities in your classroom.

Daytime/Nighttime

What affects day and night temperatures?

Materials you will need . . .

 thermal card
pencil

rubber band
masking tape

What to do . . .

1. Tape the thermal card to the pencil. Hold the pencil so that the thermal card is facing a sunny window (make sure the shade is down). Write down what you see.

2. Now pull the shade up and place the thermal card so it is facing the sunlight. Write down what you see.

3. Twist the pencil so the thermal card is now facing away from the sunlight. What happens?

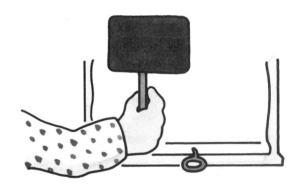

4. Imagine that the thermal card is the Earth spinning in orbit. Choose a place to live on the "Earth." When the card is facing the sunlight is it day or night for you? When will the weather be coldest for you? When will it be warmest?

Challenge

Imagine that you live on a planet where the days and nights are very short. Do you think there would be a big difference between the daytime and nighttime temperatures?

Science Process and Thinking Skills

observing

making and using models*

Materials

- thermal card
- rubber band
- pencil
- masking tape

What to Expect

This is a good activity to do on a sunny day. Students will observe a time lag in the thermal card's color change and patterns between "day" and "night." In the shade, the thermal card will look dark blue. In the sunlight, the card will look brownish yellow.

Science Background

Day and night are phenomena associated with the spin or rotation of the Earth. The sun lights half the Earth at a time, and that half continually changes with the Earth's rotation. When the portion of the Earth a person lives on is oriented toward the sun, it is daytime. When that part of the Earth is away from the sun, it is nighttime. In general, the land and water areas of the Earth gain heat energy in the daytime and lose it at night. Local weather and various climatic factors effect this general pattern.

Possible Visual Response

shade down
card blue
shade up
card yellow

Activity 1

Daytime/Nighttime
What affects day and night temperatures?

Materials you will need . . .

 thermal card   rubber band
pencil   masking tape

What to do . . .

1. Tape the thermal card to the pencil. Hold the pencil so that the thermal card is facing a sunny window (make sure the shade is down). Write down what you see.

2. Now pull the shade up and place the thermal card so it is facing the sunlight. Write down what you see.

3. Twist the pencil so the thermal card is now facing away from the sunlight. What happens?

4. Imagine that the thermal card is the Earth spinning in orbit. Choose a place to live on the "Earth." When the card is facing the sunlight is it day or night for you? When will the weather be coldest for you? When will it be warmest?

Challenge

Imagine that you live on a planet where the days and nights are very short. Do you think there would be a big difference between the daytime and nighttime temperatures?

From the ExploraCenter Activity Booklet. Copyright © 1993 Scott, Foresman and Company.

| 5 | Grade 4 |

The sun is a star. At its center, the temperature is thought to be somewhere between 10,000,000 and 20,000,000 degrees Celsius.

On Earth, we receive only a tiny amount of the energy the sun produces.

Extensions and Experiments

Use a globe to teach students about the rising and setting of the sun. Make a small paper cut-out of a person and tape it to the globe with his/her

head pointing north. Orient the globe so that it is daytime for the "person." Now slowly spin the globe and have the students predict in which direction the Earth must spin in order

for the sun to rise in the east. The students will see that the Earth rotates from west to east.

DIFFICULTY LEVEL

AVERAGE
EASY   CHALLENGING

TIME NEEDED
20–30 MINUTES

Where Are You Going?

Can you use a compass?

Materials you will need . . .

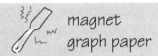
magnet
graph paper

compass
iron nail

What to do . . .

1. Place the compass at the center of a sheet of graph paper. After the needle has stopped moving, turn the compass so that the needle is pointing north. Now write the directions *north, south, east,* and *west* on your graph paper.

3. Slowly bring one end of your magnet toward the compass needle. What happened? Did you bring a north or south pole toward the needle? Now use the opposite pole of the magnet.

4. If you bring an iron nail near the compass, what happens?

Challenge

If you go for a hike through an area that has a lot of iron ore in the ground, what might happen to your compass?

2. On your graph paper, mark the direction that you would look to see the sun rise. Mark where you think the sun will set. Put an **X** on your graph paper to show where you live.

Science Process and Thinking Skills

recognizing space
relationships
inferring*

Materials

- magnet
- compass
- graph paper
- iron nail

What to Expect

🚫 Students should never bring the magnet into contact with the compass or computers.

Students with little experience using a compass may not understand that they must rotate the dial until the needle is over the **N** or "North" before they can tell direction.

As the students move the magnet around the compass, they will see that the needle orients itself so that it points to the North pole of the magnet.

Science Background

The Earth is surrounded by an invisible magnetic field. This field extends outward into space. We are not sure what produces this magnetic field. It may be caused by the movement of iron and nickel in molten form at the center of the Earth.

Possible Visual Response

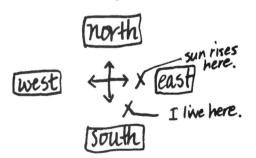

Activity

2

Where Are You Going?

Can you use a compass?

Materials you will need . . .

magnet
graph paper

compass
iron nail

What to do . . .

❶. Place the compass at the center of a sheet of graph paper. After the needle has stopped moving, turn the compass so that the needle is pointing north. Now write the directions *north, south, east,* and *west* on your graph paper.

❷. On your graph paper, mark the direction that you would look to see the sun rise. Mark where you think the sun will set. Put an **X** on your graph paper to show where you live.

❸. Slowly bring one end of your magnet toward the compass needle. What happened? Did you bring a north or south pole toward the needle? Now use the opposite pole of the magnet.

❹. If you bring an iron nail near the compass, what happens?

Challenge

If you go for a hike through an area that has a lot of iron ore in the ground, what might happen to your compass?

From the ExploraCenter Activity Booklet. Copyright © 1993 Scott, Foresman and Company.

Long ago, people navigated without using a compass. Polynesians traveled across thousands of miles of ocean guided by the positions of the stars, the angles of the sun and moon, and by studying the currents and waves and by observing migrating birds.

Extensions and Experiments

With two bar magnets, you can demonstrate that the north pole of the magnet is in fact a north-seeking pole. Suspend one magnet by a string attached to its center so it is balanced and free to rotate horizontally. Then bring the north pole of a second magnet close to it.

DIFFICULTY LEVEL

AVERAGE

EASY   CHALLENGING

TIME NEEDED

20–30 MINUTES

Make a Balloon Jet!

How can you measure time and distance?

Materials you will need . . .

long narrow balloons
stopwatch
2 chairs

plastic drinking straws
meter stick

3 meters of string
masking tape

What to do . . .

1. Put the string through the straw and then tie the ends between two chairs. Push the chairs apart until the string is stretched tightly.

2. Blow up the balloon—but don't tie it—and tape it to the straw.

3. Choose a starting point on the string and move the balloon to it. How far do you think the balloon will go when you let go of it? How long do you think it will take? Try it and see if you are correct.

Challenge

How far and how fast will the balloon travel when it is 1/2 filled with air? 3/4 filled?

Science Process and Thinking Skills

measuring
recognizing space
relationships*
identifying and controlling
variables

Materials

- long narrow balloons
- plastic drinking straws
- 3 meters of string
- stopwatch
- meter stick
- masking tape
- 2 chairs

What to Expect

The balloon jets, or rockets, will easily move across the string if the string is smooth and stretched tightly. You may wish to substitute monofilament nylon fishing line to see if it works better.

Science Background

The air in the balloon is under increased pressure when the child blows into it. This pressure pushes outward against the inside of the balloon. When the neck of the balloon opens and the air starts to move out, the end pushes and creates a force that moves the balloon forward.

Something that is as complicated as a jet engine works on the very same principles as the child's rocket balloon. Students may be surprised to learn that the fuel used by modern jet planes is common and inexpensive kerosene. The kerosene combines with air taken in the front of the engine. The kerosene burns and produces gases that are very hot and under a great deal of pressure. The gases are pushed out the rear of the jet engine and produce a reaction force (thrust) which propels the plane forward.

Activity 3

Make a Balloon Jet!

How can you measure time and distance?

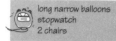
Materials you will need . . .

long narrow balloons	plastic drinking straws	3 meters of string
stopwatch	meter stick	masking tape
2 chairs		

What to do . . .

❶. Put the string through the straw and then tie the ends between two chairs. Push the chairs apart until the string is stretched tightly.

❷. Blow up the balloon—but don't tie it—and tape it to the straw.

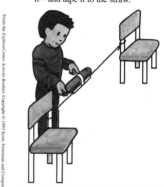

❸. Choose a starting point on the string and move the balloon to it. How far do you think the balloon will go when you let go of it? How long do you think it will take? Try it and see if you are correct.

Challenge

How far and how fast will the balloon travel when it is 1/2 filled with air? 3/4 filled?

Extensions and Experiments

You may also wish to have an assortment of balloons in various shapes and sizes available for students to test.

DIFFICULTY LEVEL
AVERAGE
EASY   CHALLENGING

TIME NEEDED
15–20 MINUTES

Life in a Drop
What's in pond water?

Materials you will need . . .

small jar with a lid
plastic dish
grass

 Fresnel lens
pond or rain water

medicine dropper
leaves

What to do . . .

1. Add some crushed grass and leaves to the water and let it sit in a warm place for about a week.

2. After one week, use the medicine dropper to put a few drops of the water on a glass dish.

3. Use the Fresnel lens to look at the water for signs of life. Draw pictures of all the living things you see.

4. Group your living things into two categories: plants and animals.

Challenge

Make your own water zoo. Keep a small jar of pond water, grass, and leaves for a few weeks. Can you get different kinds of plants and animals to grow in it?

Science Process and Thinking Skills

observing
classifying*

Materials

- small jar with a lid
- Fresnel lens
- plastic dish
- pond or rain water*
- leaves
- grass
- medicine dropper

*If you use rain water, add grass clippings, leaves, and fruit peelings.

What to Expect

The best water for this activity can be found at the edge of a pond in the vicinity of water plants. Try to collect water samples that include living plants as well as decaying material.

If the water is kept in a warm place for a few days, insect eggs will hatch on the plant material.

Science Background

If decaying plant matter in water is put in a warm place, it begins to break down. Tiny animals and plants become active, and insect eggs may also hatch. If the water is from a pond, there may be algae in it.

With a microscope, students may see one-celled *protozoa* (amoebas and paramecia) in the pond water. These creatures reproduce in a unique way—by splitting in two.

First, their nucleus splits. Then the remainder of the organism splits, producing two new organisms.

Possible Visual Response

Activity 4

Life in a Drop
What's in pond water?

Materials you will need . . .

small jar with a lid
plastic dish
grass

 Fresnel lens
pond or rain water

medicine dropper
leaves

What to do . . .

1. Add some crushed grass and leaves to the water and let it sit in a warm place for about a week.

2. After one week, use the medicine dropper to put a few drops of the water on a glass dish.

3. Use the Fresnel lens to look at the water for signs of life. Draw pictures of all the living things you see.

4. Group your living things into two categories: plants and animals.

Challenge

Make your own water zoo. Keep a small jar of pond water, grass, and leaves for a few weeks. Can you get different kinds of plants and animals to grow in it?

11   Grade 4

From the ExploraCenter Activity Booklet. Copyright © 1993 Scott, Foresman and Company.

Extensions and Experiments

With a small microscope, students will be able to find even smaller plants and animals—slipper-shaped paramecia may become visible as well as an *amoeba*, a one-celled animal that changes its shape as it moves.

DIFFICULTY LEVEL

AVERAGE

EASY   CHALLENGING

TIME NEEDED   1 WEEK

Quakes and Shakes

Can you see the earth move?

Materials you will need . . .

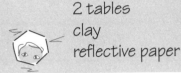

2 tables
clay
reflective paper

flashlight
index cards

What to do . . .

1. Make a model earthquake detector. First, place some clay on tables. Put a flashlight in the clay on the first table. Next to the flashlight, put an index card in the clay.

2. On the second table, place an index card in the clay. Put the reflective paper in front of the index card.

3. Shine a light beam so that it bounces off the reflective paper onto the index card on the first table. Now shake the table. What happens?

Challenge

Can you build a detector that will work if you're not there?

Science Process and Thinking Skills

making and using models
collecting and analyzing data*

Materials

- 2 tables
- flashlight
- clay
- index cards
- reflective paper

What to Expect

Students will build the monitor and find that the reflected beam greatly exaggerates the movement created by shaking the table.

Science Background

The sudden movement of horizontal layers of rock in the earth's crust can produce forces large enough to threaten life and property. Rock layers are continually being pushed together (compression) and pulled apart (tension). Usually, the forces build up over a long period of time and then are suddenly released. When this happens, rock layers may break apart, ride up over one another, or slide by each other. The earth above the layers may dip or ride up. All these effects, if sufficiently severe, can produce an earthquake.

Earthquakes that occur in California often result from the movement of crustal plates along the San Andreas fault. A crustal plate is a large moving portion of the earth's crust. The most devastating earthquake caused by this type of movement was the San Francisco earthquake of 1906.

Activity 5

Quakes and Shakes
Can you see the earth move?

Materials you will need . . .

2 tables
clay
reflective paper

flashlight
index cards

What to do . . .

❶. Make a model earthquake detector. First, place some clay on tables. Put a flashlight in the clay on the first table. Next to the flashlight, put an index card in the clay.

❷. On the second table, place an index card in the clay. Put the reflective paper in front of the index card.

❸. Shine a light beam so that it bounces off the reflective paper onto the index card on the first table. Now shake the table. What happens?

Challenge

Can you build a detector that will work if you're not there?

13   Grade 4

From the ExploraCenter Activity Booklet. Copyright © 1993 Scott, Foresman and Company.

Extensions and Experiments

Ask students to think of some ways a building can be designed to resist earthquakes.

DIFFICULTY LEVEL
AVERAGE
EASY   CHALLENGING

TIME NEEDED

40–50 MINUTES

The Color Spectrum

How bright is light?

Materials you will need . . .

diffraction grating
white and black paper
masking tape

colored paper
light source
scissors

What to do . . .

1. Cut a slot 1/2 cm wide by 5 cm long in a piece of black paper. Tape the paper to the wall so that it is in direct sunlight.

2. Now do the same with the white paper.

3. Place different colored papers behind the slots and look at the slots through the diffraction grating. Can you guess which colors in the spectrum make up the colors in the paper?

Challenge

Try this same activity, but use different types of incandescent bulbs, such as 25 watt or 75 watt. What happens?

DISCOVER THE WONDER

Module F

Science Process and Thinking Skills

inferring
observing
classifying*

Materials

- diffraction grating
- colored paper
- white and black paper
- light source
- scissors
- masking tape

What to Expect

The students will see the component colors (the colors that are actually there) against the black backround and the complementary colors (the colors that aren't there) against the white backround.

Science Background

Light is a form of energy. Not all light is the same. There are light waves, or vibrating waves of electrical and magnetic fields. Different wavelength light waves are seen as different colors. Colors are actually light waves, with red being the longest wave, and blue the shortest.

The brightness of light depends on the way it is bent and on how much is reflected or refracted. Black paper absorbs more light than white paper, so the color spectrum will appear dimmer on the black paper.

Activity 6

The Color Spectrum
How bright is light?

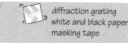
Materials you will need . . .

diffraction grating
white and black paper
masking tape

colored paper
light source
scissors

What to do . . .

1. Cut a slot 1/2 cm wide by 5 cm long in a piece of black paper. Tape the paper to the wall so that it is in direct sunlight.

2. Now do the same with the white paper.

3. Place different colored papers behind the slots and look at the slots through the diffraction grating. Can you guess which colors in the spectrum make up the colors in the paper?

Challenge

Try this same activity, but use different types of incandescent bulbs, such as 25 watt or 75 watt. What happens?

15   Grade 4

Extensions and Experiments

Ask students to choose a color and try to figure out the component colors in it.

Ask students to look at green house plant leaves and brown and orange tree leaves. How are they different? similiar?

DIFFICULTY LEVEL
AVERAGE
EASY   CHALLENGING

TIME NEEDED
30–40 MINUTES

The Floating Ball

What changes air pressure?

Materials you will need . . .

Ping Pong balls
hair dryer
stopwatch

chalk
cover goggles

What to do . . .

1. Drop the Ping Pong ball to the floor. Where does it land? Ask a friend to mark the spot with chalk.

2. Drop it again, but this time have your friend blow sideways on the ball as it leaves your hand. Did it land in a different place? Mark the spot.

3. Drop the ball a third time, but have your friend aim a hair dryer at it. Where does it hit the floor? Mark the spot.

4. How long can you keep the ball floating while you move the hair dryer up and down? in a circle? Use the stopwatch to find out.

Challenge

Can you float the ball in the air by using a hair dryer? Can you move the ball from place to place as it floats?

Science Process and Thinking Skills

observing
experimenting*

Materials

- Ping Pong balls
- hair dryer
- stopwatch
- chalk
- cover goggles

What to Expect

This is a good group activity. Students will need access to electrical outlets at widely spaced locations around the room. If this poses a problem, you may want to carry out this activity as a demonstration involving various students as "science helpers" at the front of the room.

Science Background

Objects move as a result of pushes and pulls. In this activity, a hair dryer directs the flow of air toward a Ping Pong ball. The Ping Pong ball is supported because the nozzle of the hair dryer keeps the moving air together for a short while after it leaves the internal fan. This permits students to produce what is in effect a column of air that can be directed accurately over short distances. The air splits at the bottom of the ball and moves quickly along its sides. This reduces the air pressure at each side, and keeps the ball from moving out of the air stream.

Airplanes fly as a result of the movement of air across their wings. The tops of wings are designed so that air moving over them has to move along a longer curved path than air moving along the bottom. This path can be increased or decreased by using the wing flaps,

Activity 7

The Floating Ball
What changes air pressure?

Materials you will need . . .

Ping Pong balls
hair dryer
stopwatch

chalk
cover goggles

What to do . . .

1. Drop the Ping Pong ball to the floor. Where does it land? Ask a friend to mark the spot with chalk.

2. Drop it again, but this time have your friend blow sideways on the ball as it leaves your hand. Did it land in a different place? Mark the spot.

3. Drop the ball a third time, but have your friend aim a hair dryer at it. Where does it hit the floor? Mark the spot.

4. How long can you keep the ball floating while you move the hair dryer up and down? in a circle? Use the stopwatch to find out.

Challenge

Can you float the ball in the air by using a hair dryer? Can you move the ball from place to place as it floats?

or *ailerons.* As long as the air travels a longer path across the top of the wings, the air pressure is reduced. This causes a force, called *lift,* to push the wings and the plane upward.

Extensions and Experiments

Ask students to do this activity with a balloon. They will find that the balloon is so light that it will float in the air column a

considerable distance above the hair dryer nozzle.

DIFFICULTY LEVEL
AVERAGE
EASY   CHALLENGING

TIME NEEDED
15–20 MINUTES

Salty Solutions

Can you make salt crystals?

Materials you will need . . .

warm water
table salt
2 clear plastic saucers

plastic drinking glass
tablespoon
Fresnel lens   overhead projector

What to do . . .

❶. Fill the drinking glass halfway with warm water. Now add as much salt as you can in the water, until no more will dissolve. Stir the water as you add salt.

❷. Pour water from the glass onto each saucer so the bottoms of the saucers are covered.

❸. Put one saucer in a warm place and one in a colder place. What happens after three days? seven days? two weeks?

❹. Use the Fresnel lens to look at the saucers each day, and write down what you see. What is left on the saucer after the water is gone?

Challenge

When ocean water dries up, does the salt dry up too? Invent a "thought experiment" (an imaginary experiment that you could do if you had all the equipment you needed) that would test your idea.

Science Process and Thinking Skills

observing*
experimenting

Materials

- warm water
- plastic drinking glass
- table salt
- tablespoon
- 2 clear glass saucers
- overhead projector
- Fresnel lens

What to Expect

The amount of salt that can be dissolved in the water will depend on how warm the water is and how vigorously the students stir in the salt. You may want to create your own highly concentrated salt water solution by using hot water. After it cools, you may dispense small amounts to each group.

The students will see a white residue left behind on the saucer when the water evaporates. This residue includes the salt that was previously dissolved as well as salts and other substances that are in tap water.

With an overhead projector, project light through the glass saucers at the end of the experiment. Students will see the shapes of the crystals that were formed.

Science Background

When water evaporates, it leaves a solution that contains dissolved substances left behind in a crystalline form. A *crystal* is a solid in which the atoms or molecules are arranged in a pattern. Table salt consists of small crystals of a mineral called *halite*. The size of a crystal that forms depends on various factors, including the speed with which evaporation occurred. Small crystals

Activity
8

Salty Solutions
Can you make salt crystals?

Materials you will need . . .

warm water
table salt
2 clear plastic saucers

plastic drinking glass
tablespoon
Fresnel lens

overhead projector

What to do . . .

1. Fill the drinking glass halfway with warm water. Now add as much salt as you can in the water, until no more will dissolve. Stir the water as you add salt.

2. Pour water from the glass onto each saucer so the bottoms of the saucers are covered.

3. Put one saucer in a warm place and one in a colder place. What happens after three days? seven days? two weeks?

4. Use the Fresnel lens to look at the saucers each day, and write down what you see. What is left on the saucer after the water is gone?

Challenge

When ocean water dries up, does the salt dry up too? Invent a "thought experiment" (an imaginary experiment that you could do if you had all the equipment you needed) that would test your idea.

form when a liquid is rapidly cooled. Crystals are commonly found in nature. Quartz crystals form when the mineral *silica* has dissolved in water. Some quartz crystals can become very large if the water containing the silica evaporates over a long period of time. Some crystals found in South America weigh thousands of kilograms.

Extensions and Experiments

Ask students to locate the Great Salt Lake (Utah) and the Dead Sea (Israel) on the map and then do some reading about the unique properties of the water in both locations. You

can explain to students that it is easy to float in these waters since the water is very dense due to the high concentration of salt left behind after the surface water evaporates.

DIFFICULTY LEVEL

AVERAGE

EASY   CHALLENGING

TIME NEEDED

2 WEEKS

Model Making

Can you build a model of Earth?

Materials you will need . . .

Ping Pong ball
3 colors of clay

What to do . . .

❶. Pretend a Ping Pong ball is the Earth's core. Stick globs of clay on it.

❷. Can you slide one glob across the ball, without removing it?

❸. What happens when one glob slides into another?

Challenge

Build a model of the Earth's plates using construction paper, glue, and a large ball. Make sure you show how one plate slides under another.

From the *ExploraCenter Activity Booklet*. Copyright © 1993 Scott, Foresman and Company.

Teacher Notes

Science Process and Thinking Skills

making and using models*

Materials

- Ping Pong ball
- 3 colors of clay

What to Expect

As students push the clay around, they will notice one color hitting up against another. Sometimes one color will push over or shoot under another. Other times different colors of clay will mix together a bit and ridges will form. These ridges, if made of earth rather than clay, would then form mountains.

Science Background

The surface of the Earth is formed by a series of plates on which all continents lie. The plates float on the Earth's inner core of molten rock. When plates meet, usually one slips under the other. The area where they meet is called the *subduction zone.*

If the plates meet and neither slips under, or subducts, then both will begin to rise and mountains form. The Arabian plate (India is located on it) has, for hundreds of thousands of years, pushed up against the Eurasian plate (where

Model Making
Can you build a model of Earth?

Materials you will need . . .

Ping Pong ball
3 colors of clay

What to do . . .

❶. Pretend a Ping Pong ball is the Earth's core. Stick globs of clay on it.

❷. Can you slide one glob across the ball, without removing it?

❸. What happens when one glob slides into another?

Challenge

Build a model of the Earth's plates using construction paper, glue, and a large ball. Make sure you show how one plate slides under another.

21   Grade 4

From the *ExploraCenter Activity Booklet.* Copyright © 1993 Scott, Foresman and Company.

china is located). Where these plates meet, the Himalayan mountains formed.

Possible Visual Response

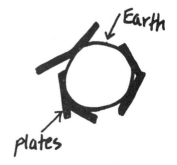

Extensions and Experiments

Ask students to try to find out where new rock is forming on the Earth. You can explain that new rock is forming through volcanic activity.

DIFFICULTY LEVEL AVERAGE EASY CHALLENGING

TIME NEEDED  15–20 MINUTES

From the *ExploraCenter Activity Booklet.* Copyright © 1993 Scott, Foresman and Company.

Cool It!

Can you cool the thermal card?

Materials you will need . . .

stopwatch
water
plastic bowl

thermal card
sealable bag

What to do . . .

1. Look at the thermal card. What colors do you see?

2. Place the card in a sealable bag and put it into a bowl filled with warm water for two minutes. Write down what you see.

3. Now take the thermal card out of the bag. What happens when you splash cold water on it? Write down what you see.

Challenge

Do you think the outside of your body heats up when you exercise? How can you use the thermal card to find out?

Science Process and Thinking Skills

predicting*
interpreting data

Materials

- thermal card
- water
- plastic bowl
- stopwatch
- sealable bag

What to Expect

The thermal card will show changes in color when it gets warmer and then gets cooler. These changes will be most pronounced when cold and warm water are alternately splashed on the card.

Science Background

The thermal card is covered with a coating that reacts to differences in temperature. Since the warm water temperature will probably be higher than the room temperature, the card will probably turn brown. The cool water will probably turn the thermal card green or blue.

One temperature scale is called the *Fahrenheit* scale. It was developed by Gabriel Fahrenheit, who named the lowest temperature he could by mixing ice, salt, and water at 0 degrees. On his scale, the temperature at which ice melts or water freezes is 32 degrees, the average temperature of a human body is 98.6 degrees, and the boiling temperature

Possible Visual Response

① blue

② yellow

③ yellow with green dots

From the ExploraCenter Activity Booklet. Copyright © 1993 Scott, Foresman and Company.

Activity 10

Cool It!

Can you cool the thermal card?

Materials you will need . . .

stopwatch
water
plastic bowl

thermal card
sealable bag

What to do . . .

❶. Look at the thermal card. What colors do you see?

❷. Place the card in a sealable bag and put it into a bowl filled with warm water for two minutes. Write down what you see.

❸. Now take the thermal card out of the bag. What happens when you splash cold water on it? Write down what you see.

Challenge

Do you think the outside of your body heats up when you exercise? How can you use the thermal card to find out?

23   Grade 4

---

of water is 212 degrees. Fahrenheit actually said that human body temperature was 96 degrees. But his thermometers were not as accurate as the ones we have now. The inventor of the *Centigrade* or *Celsius* scale was Anders Celsius. On his scale, water freezes at 0 degrees and boils at 100 degrees.

Extensions and Experiments

Ask students to compare the color changes that occur when a group of them simultaneously place their cards between their hands.

DIFFICULTY LEVEL

AVERAGE
EASY   CHALLENGING

TIME NEEDED

20–30 MINUTES

Pop Your Top!
Can you make a model volcano?

Materials you will need . . .

3 plastic film containers
  with lids
cover goggles

white vinegar
teaspoon

baking powder
tablespoon

What to do . . .

1. Make a chart with columns for 1/2 teaspoon, 1 teaspoon, and 1 1/2 teaspoons, of baking powder.

2. Put on your cover goggles. Add a tablespoon of vinegar to each container. Then place 1/2 teaspoon of baking powder in one container, 1 teaspoon in another, and 1 1/2 teaspoons in the third.

3. Quickly put the lid on the containers. Make sure your face is not near them. What happens in each container? Write about what you see.

Challenge

Can you think of a way to do this activity without using vinegar and baking powder?

Science Process and Thinking Skills

inferring*
experimenting
identifying and controlling
variables

Materials

- 3 plastic film containers with lids
- white vinegar
- baking powder
- teaspoon
- tablespoon
- cover goggles

What to Expect

🚫 Students should wear cover goggles. Students should not look down at the top of the container because the lid may be launched a few feet in the air.

You will need to use film containers that have a pop-off lids. The particular "recipe" needed to produce enough gas to pop off the lid will depend on the freshness of the baking powder and vinegar. Students should work very quickly to cover the top of the container because the fizzing will begin as soon as the vinegar touches the baking powder.

Science Background

Vinegar and baking powder react to form various products, including carbon dioxide gas. When molten rock (magma) from below the surface of the earth flows upward, large amounts of gas are released. If the opening from which the molten rock usually flows to the land surface is blocked by rock, pressure is created. The enormous pressure of the magma against the blocked opening can cause explosions that hurl rocks, molten rock, volcanic dust, and other particles into the air.

Pop Your Top!
Can you make a model volcano?

Materials you will need . . .

3 plastic film containers with lids cover goggles	white vinegar teaspoon	baking powder tablespoon

What to do . . .

❶. Make a chart with columns for 1/2 teaspoon, 1 teaspoon, and 1 1/2 teaspoons, of baking powder.

❷. Put on your cover goggles. Add a tablespoon of vinegar to each container. Then place 1/2 teaspoon of baking powder in one container, 1 teaspoon in another, and 1 1/2 teaspoons in the third.

❸. Quickly put the lid on the containers. Make sure your face is not near them. What happens in each container? Write about what you see.

Challenge

Can you think of a way to do this activity without using vinegar and baking powder?

The "Ring of Fire" is an area around the edge of the Pacific plate (a portion of the Earth's crust that is under the Pacific Ocean) that has over 300 volcanoes. This area goes along the west coast of North and South America and along the eastern coast of Asia, through Japan, and extends south to New Zealand.

Extensions and Experiments

Students can demonstrate the pressure created by baking powder and vinegar reaction by shaping a cork stopper to fit a glass soda bottle. They can wrap the bottle in a cloth towel, and fill it about a third of the way with vinegar. If they add a few teaspoons of baking powder to bottle, and put the cork on, it will pop off due to the pressure of the carbon dioxide gas.

DIFFICULTY LEVEL

AVERAGE
EASY CHALLENGING

TIME NEEDED

30–40 MINUTES

Bouncing Beams

Can you see air pollution?

Materials you will need . . .

reflective paper
black paper
cover goggles

flashlight
2 chalk-covered erasers

What to do . . .

1. Shine the flashlight at a wall across the room. Where does the beam hit the wall? Can you see the beam itself or just the place where it hits the wall?

2. Now clap the erasers together near the end of the flashlight. Can you see the beam more clearly now?

3. Hold up the reflective paper and aim the flashlight at it. Move the reflective paper so that the light hits the wall at a different spot. Which way do you think the beams will move?

4. Now clap the eraser near the reflective paper. Draw the light beam changing direction. Was your guess correct?

Challenge

What do you think would happen to air pollution over a city that got little rain and no wind?

Science Process and Thinking Skills

observing
experimenting*

Materials

- reflective paper
- flashlight
- black paper
- 2 chalk-covered erasers
- cover goggles

What to Expect

This activity will require a darkened room. This is a good group activity. You may wish to spend some time getting groups organized and deciding which groups will shine the flashlight. Collect chalk-covered erasers before the activity starts and distribute them only when groups are ready to use them.

Science Background

Not all air pollution is visible. Some of the most dangerous forms of air pollution are invisible—for example, carbon monoxide from automobile exhaust. When we notice smog or haze in the atmosphere we are usually seeing the effect of small bits of particulate matter that are suspended in the air. Light that passes through air that has a lot of particulate matter is scattered, so we receive less direct light than we normally do.

Sometimes a layer of warm air traps cooler air underneath it, causing a phenomenon called a *temperature inversion*. Trapped polluted air remains in place as additional pollutants are added by automobiles and industrial exhausts. The longer the air is trapped, the worse the pollution gets.

Humans are not the only source of air pollution. The eruption of vol-

---

Bouncing Beams
Can you see air pollution?

Materials you will need . . .

reflective paper
black paper
cover goggles

flashlight
2 chalk-covered erasers

What to do . . .

1. Shine the flashlight at a wall across the room. Where does the beam hit the wall? Can you see the beam itself or just the place where it hits the wall?

2. Now clap the erasers together near the end of the flashlight. Can you see the beam more clearly now?

3. Hold up the reflective paper and aim the flashlight at it. Move the reflective paper so that the light hits the wall at a different spot. Which way do you think the beams will move?

4. Now clap the eraser near the reflective paper. Draw the light beam changing direction. Was your guess correct?

Challenge

What do you think would happen to air pollution over a city that got little rain and no wind?

From the ExploraCenter Activity Booklet. Copyright © 1993 Scott, Foresman and Company.

canoes puts a great deal of pollution in the air, as do forest fires.

Extensions and Experiments

Ask students to name some of the causes of air and water pollution. Then ask them if they can think of any ways to prevent them.

DIFFICULTY LEVEL

AVERAGE

EASY   CHALLENGING

TIME NEEDED

20–30 MINUTES

Cool Cards
Does cool air sink?

Materials you will need . . .

thermal card
ice cubes
sealable plastic bag

meter stick
heat source

What to do . . .

1. What color is the thermal card? Hold the thermal card near a heat source. What color is the card now?

2. Now place the ice cube in the bag and hold it 5 cm above the card. Do you see any places where cold air is reaching the card?

3. Now hold the card near a heat source again and then hold it 5 cm above the ice cube. What color is the card?

Challenge

Use the thermal card to find out if the air near a light bulb moves in currents. Make sure the thermal card is cool.

Science Process and Thinking Skills

inferring
predicting*

Materials

- thermal card
- ice cubes
- heat source
- meter stick
- sealable plastic bag

What to Expect

If the students can't keep the water from dripping on the card, they can use plastic sandwich bags to hold the cube. Students will see that the thermal card cools in specific locations because streams of cold air descend from the ice cube. To get the best results, make sure that the thermal card is fully warmed before students place the ice cube above it.

Science Background

Air that is cooled is more dense than its surroundings. Consequently, it sinks. As a result of this process, warmer air is pushed up, creating a convection current. Since the thermal card is sensitive to temperature changes, it will respond when a stream of cold air descends from the ice cube. Students can see the opposite effect by holding a thermal card above a desk lamp. The rise of heated air is caused by air that is cooling sinking and displacing the hot air.

A hot air balloon rises because as the air in the balloon is heated, the less dense air surrounding it sinks down and under it, lifting the balloon. In 1783, the Montgolfier brothers (Joseph and Jacques) demonstrated that hot air balloons could carry people. In 1785, two other men flew across the English channel in a hot air balloon.

Cool Cards
Does cool air sink?

Materials you will need . . .

thermal card
ice cubes
sealable plastic bag

meter stick
heat source

What to do . . .

❶. What color is the thermal card? Hold the thermal card near a heat source. What color is the card now?

❷. Now place the ice cube in the bag and hold it 5 cm above the card. Do you see any places where cold air is reaching the card?

❸. Now hold the card near a heat source again and then hold it 5 cm above the ice cube. What color is the card?

Challenge

Use the thermal card to find out if the air near a light bulb moves in currents. Make sure the thermal card is cool.

29   **Grade 4**

Nowadays, people use hot air balloons for recreation.

Extensions and Experiments

If your classroom is heated or cooled by radiators or air conditioning, you can encourage students to see if they can detect a temperature

difference when they place a thermal card near the ceiling (they can tape the card to a broomstick), and near the floor.

Students can also make bubbles using a bubble "wand" and soap, to see if they can find areas in the room where air currents exist.

DIFFICULTY LEVEL

AVERAGE

EASY   CHALLENGING

TIME NEEDED

30–40 MINUTES

Free Fall

What affects a parachute's fall?

Materials you will need . . .

stopwatch	coffee filters	chalk
4 strings of equal length	scissors	meter stick
chair	masking tape	

What to do . . .

1. Tape the strings to the edges of a coffee filter and tie their ends together to make a parachute. Tie a piece of chalk to the ends of the string.

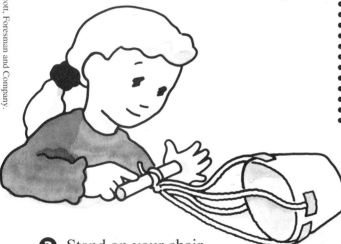

2. Stand on your chair and carefully drop the parachute so that it falls, fully opened and slowly.

3. Have a friend measure the distance from where you dropped the parachute and use the stopwatch to time the drop.

4. Do this several times. Are the times the same?

Challenge

Design different types of parachutes by experimenting with varying the numbers of strings and weights of chalk, and by cutting a small hole in the center of the coffee filter.

Science Process and Thinking Skills

predicting
measuring
identifying and controlling
variables*

Materials

- stopwatch
- coffee filters
- chalk
- 4 strings of equal length
- scissors
- meter stick
- chair
- masking tape

What to Expect

Tying the strings to the edges of the coffee filter may be difficult for some students. You may want to provide a hole punch that students can use to make holes along the edge of the filters. To minimize confusion in the classroom and assure safety, you may want to schedule the parachute tests. Each group can come to the front of the room to demonstrate their designs one at a time. If the weather is appropriate, this is an excellent outdoor activity.

Science Background

If there were no atmosphere surrounding the Earth, any object dropped from above the surface would increase its speed at the rate of 32 feet per second. However, the atmosphere causes falling objects to experience air resistance which slows them down. A parachute has a large surface, so there is even more air resistence. Parachutes have been designed for a variety of purposes.

Modern parachutes are designed to automatically open when they reach a certain altitude. This is a safety precaution. In the event the

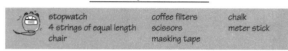

Free Fall
What affects a parachute's fall?

Materials you will need . . .

stopwatch
4 strings of equal length
chair

coffee filters
scissors
masking tape

chalk
meter stick

What to do . . .

1. Tape the strings to the edges of a coffee filter and tie their ends together to make a parachute. Tie a piece of chalk to the ends of the string.

2. Stand on your chair and carefully drop the parachute so that it falls, fully opened and slowly.

3. Have a friend measure the distance from where you dropped the parachute and use the stopwatch to time the drop.

4. Do this several times. Are the times the same?

Challenge

Design different types of parachutes by experimenting with varying the numbers of strings and weights of chalk, and by cutting a small hole in the center of the coffee filter.

31   Grade 4

parachutist forgets to open the chute on time or gets injured as he or she leaves the plane, the chute will still open. Skydivers usually jump out of

aircraft with two parachutes strapped to their bodies—one is their regular parachute and the other is a smaller second parachute to use if there are problems with the first.

Extensions and Experiments

If you teach near a military base or a civilian airfield used by skydivers, you can invite them to visit your classroom and bring a parachute along for the students to see.

Ask students to try to design parachutes that will drop faster.

DIFFICULTY LEVEL

AVERAGE

EASY   CHALLENGING

TIME NEEDED

20–30 MINUTES

Underwater Surprises

Does water have pressure?

Materials you will need . . .

bucket
water
long rubber gloves

What to do . . .

1. Add water to the bucket until it is about 3/4 full.

2. Stick one hand in the water, just below the surface. Can you feel the water pressing on your hand?

3. Now push your hand to the bottom of the bucket. What do you feel?

4. Remove your hand from the water. Blow into the rubber glove until it is full. Then push the glove down into the water with the open side down. Is there air or water in the glove?

5. Squeeze the glove. What happens?

Challenge

Air and water apply pressure to whatever is in them. How can you measure the amount of air pressure caused by the atmosphere?

Science Process and Thinking Skills

inferring
experimenting
communicating*

Materials

- bucket
- water
- long rubber gloves

What to Expect

You may wish to have students try this activity over a sink. If weather permits, this is an excellent activity to do outdoors.

Students will see that the glove maintains its shape under water. Be sure that they place it under the water with the open side down, or the air will escape and the glove will collapse.

Science Background

Water pushes on all things under its surface. The amount of force applied to a surface area is called *pressure.* The deeper one goes in water, the more the pressure increases. When a glove filled with air is pushed straight down in the water, the pressure of the water filling the glove is balanced by the pressure of the air that is already inside the glove. When students squeeze the glove, they increase the pressure of the air inside the glove so the air is forced into the water.

How can a submarine keep from being crushed in the ocean? Submarines are able to resist this pressure because they are pressurized internally with air. This internal pressure presses against the inside of the hull and balances the water pressure pressing inward. The first submarines, invented in the 1600s, couldn't descend very far because

---

Activity 15

Underwater Surprises
Does water have pressure?

Materials you will need . . .

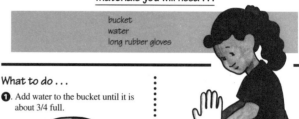

bucket
water
long rubber gloves

What to do . . .

❶. Add water to the bucket until it is about 3/4 full.

❷. Stick one hand in the water, just below the surface. Can you feel the water pressing on your hand?

❸. Now push your hand to the bottom of the bucket. What do you feel?

❹. Remove your hand from the water. Blow into the rubber glove until it is full. Then push the glove down into the water with the open side down. Is there air or water in the glove?

❺. Squeeze the glove. What happens?

Challenge

Air and water apply pressure to whatever is in them. How can you measure the amount of air pressure caused by the atmosphere?

33   Grade 4

---

they were made of wood and animal hide. One of the deepest descents in modern time was made by a special diving vessel called a *bathyscaphe.* It carried people 6 miles (about 9 1/2 km) below the ocean's surface.

Extensions and Experiments

Students can read about what happens when underwater divers come to the surface too quickly. This condition is called the "bends" and is caused when our bodies do not have enough

time to compensate for a rapid change in pressure. Students can locate information about this problem by reading about underwater diving, or scuba diving.

DIFFICULTY LEVEL

AVERAGE

EASY   CHALLENGING

TIME NEEDED

15–20 MINUTES

Planets—Hot and Cold

How hot does a planet get?

Materials you will need . . .

thermal card
desk lamp
9 index cards

What to do . . .

1. On the index cards, write the names of all nine planets in the solar system. Put them in the correct order from the "sun" (the lamp).

2. Now put the thermal card at the Earth's location. Turn the lamp on and move the thermal card toward it until you start to see changes. What happens?

3. After a few minutes, put the thermal card in a cool place until it returns to its original color.

4. Now put the thermal card near the lamp, but this time tilt it so the top half is pointing away from the "sun." Do you see any changes?

Challenge

Try this activity outside. See whether the surface of the thermal card changes more when it is pointed toward the sun or away from the sun.

Science Process and Thinking Skills

observing
interpreting data*

Materials

- thermal card
- desk lamp
- 9 index cards

What to Expect

The planet names and their relative positions, in the proper order from the sun, are as follows: Mercury, Venus, Earth, Mars, Jupiter, Saturn, Uranus, Neptune, Pluto.

Students will see that the whole thermal card heats up and changes color when it is directly facing the sun. When the top of the card is inclined away from the lamp, the top will heat less and only a portion of the card will change color.

Science Background

The main reasons for the seasons on Earth have little to do with whether the Earth is close or far from the sun during its orbit. The seasons are caused by the inclination (angle of tilt) of the Earth relative to the plane of its orbit. As the Earth revolves, its axis is pointed toward the sun for part of the year and away from the sun for part of the year.

Humans adapt by varying the amount of clothing they wear, and by heating or cooling their buildings.

Possible Visual Response

yellow
green

Activity
16

Planets—Hot and Cold
How hot does a planet get?

Materials you will need . . .

thermal card
desk lamp
9 index cards

What to do . . .

1. On the index cards, write the names of all nine planets in the solar system. Put them in the correct order from the "sun" (the lamp).

2. Now put the thermal card at the Earth's location. Turn the lamp on and move the thermal card toward it until you start to see changes. What happens?

3. After a few minutes, put the thermal card in a cool place until it returns to its original color.

4. Now put the thermal card near the lamp, but this time tilt it so the top half is pointing away from the "sun." Do you see any changes?

Challenge

Try this activity outside. See whether the surface of the thermal card changes more when it is pointed toward the sun or away from the sun.

From the ExploraCenter Activity Booklet. Copyright © 1993 Scott, Foresman and Company.

35   Grade 4

Bears and hedgehogs react to severe winter weather by hibernating. While they hibernate, their body functions slow down (heart rate, breathing, etc.) and they use very little energy. The energy their bodies use comes from excess fat accumulated during the feeding periods—spring, summer, and fall.

Extensions and Experiments

Use a globe to show the students that the Earth maintains a tilt of a little more than 23 degrees as it revolves around the sun. Ask one child to represent the sun. Move the Earth in orbit around the child while it is held at a 23-degree angle. Students should be able to tell when they will have summer and winter.

DIFFICULTY LEVEL

EASY

AVERAGE
CHALLENGING

TIME NEEDED

40–50 MINUTES

Lens Laboratory

What can you learn from lenses?

Materials you will need . . .

Fresnel lens
meter stick

flashlight
black and white paper

What to do . . .

❶. Put your lens on a sheet of black paper and shine a light through it. Now leave the light where it is and move the lens toward and away from it. What happens?

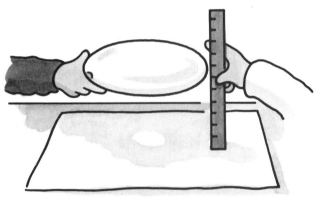

❸. Measure the distance from the center of the lens to the bright spot on the paper. What do you think this is called?

❹. Make a small drawing on a sheet of white paper. Now move the lens close to the paper and look at your drawing. What do you see?

❷. Adjust the lens and the flashlight so a bright spot appears on the black paper. What do you think this is?

Challenge

Can you build your own telescope?

Science Process and Thinking Skills

inferring
experimenting
making and using models*

Materials

- Fresnel lens
- flashlight
- black and white paper
- meter stick

What to Expect

Students will discover that their lens will bring light rays together to form a bright spot, or a *focal point*, on the black paper. They will also measure *focal length*. When they move their lens back and forth over the diagram, they will see the image change. When the lens is brought very close to the object, students will see an enlarged and erect image.

Science Background

A lens is a transparent material that affects the path of light rays that travel through it. If a lens is thicker at the center than at the edges, it is called a *convex* lens. The lens in the ExploraCenter is a Fresnel lens. If you examine it carefully, you will notice a pattern of circles. This pattern causes the same effect as a convex lens. Both lenses bring light rays together.

The human eye has a convex lens. Humans are able to focus on objects that are close as well as distant because muscles around the lens in our eyes adjust automatically. These changes vary the thickness of the center of the lens and permit us to focus clearly. Microscopes and telescopes also use convex lenses.

Activity
17

Lens Laboratory
What can you learn from lenses?

Materials you will need . . .

Fresnel lens
meter stick

flashlight
black and white paper

What to do . . .

❶. Put your lens on a sheet of black paper and shine a light through it. Now leave the light where it is and move the lens toward and away from it. What happens?

❸. Measure the distance from the center of the lens to the bright spot on the paper. What do you think this is called?

❹. Make a small drawing on a sheet of white paper. Now move the lens close to the paper and look at your drawing. What do you see?

Challenge

Can you build your own telescope?

❷. Adjust the lens and the flashlight so a bright spot appears on the black paper. What do you think this is?

From the ExploraCenter Activity Booklet. Copyright © 1993 Scott, Foresman and Company.

37   **Grade 4**

Extensions and Experiments

Students can create small magnifying lenses by placing drops of water on plastic wrap. They will see that the drop is thicker at the center than at the edge, and will have magnify-ing properties. You can ask them to examine words and pictures with their water drop magnifier.

DIFFICULTY LEVEL

AVERAGE

EASY   CHALLENGING

TIME NEEDED

40–50 MINUTES

From the ExploraCenter Activity Booklet. Copyright © 1993 Scott, Foresman and Company.

Temperatures High and Low!

What can the thermal card do?

Materials you will need . . .

empty aquarium
bowl of warm water
thermal card

bowl of ice cubes
cardboard lid for the aquarium
stopwatch

string
masking tape

What to do . . .

1. Tape the thermal card to a piece of string. Hang it from the lid inside the aquarium for two minutes. What color is the card? Lower the card to the bottom of the aquarium.

2. Now remove the lid, and put the bowl of ice cubes on the bottom of the aquarium. Repeat Step 1, but don't touch the card to the ice cubes.

3. Remove the bowl of ice cubes and place the bowl of warm water on the bottom of the aquarium. Repeat Step 1. What happened to the color of the thermal card?

Challenge

What happens if you put the ice cubes at one end of the aquarium and a bowl of warm water at the other end?

Science Process and Thinking Skills

measuring*
collecting and interpreting
data
inferring

Materials

- empty aquarium*
- bowl of ice cubes
- bowl of warm water
- cardboard lid for the aquarium
- thermal card
- stopwatch
- string
- masking tape

*you can use a large empty mayonnaise jar.

What to Expect

As the students carry out this activity, be sure that they allow sufficient time for the thermal card to respond to temperature differences.

Science Background

Although the temperature of the air is usually measured with a thermometer, the thermal card can indicate temperature differences within the aquarium by changing color. In general, cold air is more dense than warm air and will either sink or remain at the bottom of the aquarium. Warmer air will rise to the top of the aquarium.

During weather forecasts, you hear the terms "low pressure area" or "high pressure area." These are caused by the uneven heating of the

earth's surface and the convection currents that are produced as a result. A low pressure area is created when the earth heats enough to make air rise. This area of rising air is a low pressure area. Sinking cold-

er air produces a high pressure area. When cold air moves through an area that has warmer air, the warm air will rise. This is called a *cold front.*

Temperatures High and Low!
What can the thermal card do?

Materials you will need . . .

empty aquarium	bowl of ice cubes	string
bowl of warm water	cardboard lid for the aquarium	masking tape
thermal card	stopwatch	

What to do . . .

1. Tape the thermal card to a piece of string. Hang it from the lid inside the aquarium for two minutes. What color is the card? Lower the card to the bottom of the aquarium.

2. Now remove the lid, and put the bowl of ice cubes on the bottom of the aquarium. Repeat Step 1, but don't touch the card to the ice cubes.

3. Remove the bowl of ice cubes and place the bowl of warm water on the bottom of the aquarium. Repeat Step 1. What happened to the color of the thermal card?

Challenge

What happens if you put the ice cubes at one end of the aquarium and a bowl of warm water at the other end?

Extensions and Experiments

Ask students to think of a way to demonstrate temperature changes when cold air and warm air interact.

Possible Visual Response

① blue

② blue green

③ brown

DIFFICULTY LEVEL

AVERAGE
EASY   CHALLENGING

TIME NEEDED
40–50 MINUTES

Hot and Cold

Can you guess the weather?

Materials you will need . . .

graph paper
thermometer
thermal card

From the *ExploraCenter Activity Booklet* Copyright © 1993 Scott, Foresman and Company.

What to do . . .

1. Can you guess what the highest and lowest outdoor temperatures will be in the next two weeks? Make a graph and write down your guesses.

3. After two weeks, find the highest and the lowest temperatures. Were your guesses correct?

Challenge

Can you think of a way to use the thermal card to make a cold day seem warm and a warm day seem cold?

2. Use the thermometer to take the temperature outside each day at the same time. Write down your readings and whether it was cloudy, foggy, raining, or snowing.

Science Process and Thinking Skills

collecting and analyzing data
measuring
predicting*

Materials

- graph paper
- thermometer
- thermal card

What to Expect

If the students have not used graph paper before, this is a good introductory activity. As they make their graphs, be sure that they label the vertical and horizontal axis (temperature and days, respectively), title their graph, and place their temperature data at the proper location.

Science Background

The Celsius (Centigrade) thermometer is the principal tool used by scientists to measure temperature. On the Celsius thermometer, freezing is 0 degrees and the boiling temperature of water is 100 degrees. Day to day variations in outdoor temperature can result from cloud cover, the arrival of warm and cold fronts, general climate, and other factors.

Scientists who study weather and make forecasts about the arrival of warm and cold fronts are called *meteorologists*. Anyone interested in becoming a meteorologist must be a good observer and be interested in both science and mathematics.

From the *ExploraCenter Activity Booklet*. Copyright © 1993 Scott, Foresman and Company.

Hot and Cold
Can you guess the weather?

Materials you will need . . .

graph paper
thermometer
thermal card

What to do . . .

1. Can you guess what the highest and lowest outdoor temperatures will be in the next two weeks? Make a graph and write down your guesses.

2. Use the thermometer to take the temperature outside each day at the same time. Write down your readings and whether it was cloudy, foggy, raining, or snowing.

3. After two weeks, find the highest and the lowest temperatures. Were your guesses correct?

Challenge

Can you think of a way to use the thermal card to make a cold day seem warm and a warm day seem cold?

Extensions and Experiments

Give students world maps and ask them to try to find the three major climatic zones on our planet. The "temperate" zone is from 30 degrees to 60 degrees latitude. The "tropical zone" is from 30 degrees latitude to the equator. The "polar zone" is from the north or south pole to 60 degrees latitude.

From the *ExploraCenter Activity Booklet*. Copyright © 1993 Scott, Foresman and Company.

DIFFICULTY LEVEL

AVERAGE

EASY   CHALLENGING

TIME NEEDED

2 WEEKS

Make It Sink!

How do rocks form?

Materials you will need . . .

2 liter, clear bottle with a top
1 cup of aquarium gravel
stopwatch

1 cup of aquarium sand
blue food coloring

What to do . . .

1. Add the sand and gravel to the empty bottle and then fill it about 3/4 full of water. Dye the water blue and put the cap on the bottle.

2. Turn the bottle upside down and then right side up. Let the sand and gravel settle to the bottom. Use a stopwatch to time how long they take to settle.

3. Which settles to the bottom first? Make a drawing to show this.

4. Now repeat the activity. What happens?

Challenge

Imagine that you are a geologist who discovers a cliff that is made up of layers of rocks with fossils. Which layers do you think would have the oldest fossils? the youngest?

From the *ExploraCenter Activity Booklet.* Copyright © 1993 Scott, Foresman and Company.

Activity 20

Teacher Notes

Science Process and Thinking Skills

observing
predicting
recognizing time and space*

Materials

- 2 liter, clear bottle with a top
- 1 cup of aquarium sand
- 1 cup of aquarium gravel*
- blue food coloring
- stopwatch

*You can also use clay

What to Expect

Students will find that although the water is cloudy at first, the sand and gravel will settle to the bottom. Students will see that the gravel will settle first, no matter how many times they repeat the activity.

Science Background

Soil particles and rock fragments are constantly added to streams, ponds, lakes, and the oceans by rain water that moves across the land. These materials are temporarily suspended in the water, but eventually settle to the bottom. Over a long period of time, the accumulating weight of these materials presses down and forms sedimentary rocks. By studying sedimentary rocks, students can learn a great deal about the land area that borders the body of water under which the rocks formed.

In this demonstration, students will see coarse particles of gravel settle before the sand does. In layered sedimentary rocks, the material in the top layers is made of finer particles than the lower rock layers.

Water currents will affect where sedimentation takes place since moving water carries sediments. Sometimes underwater avalanches are caused when layers of sand and

---

Activity 20

Make It Sink!

How do rocks form?

_____ Materials you will need . . . _____

2 liter, clear bottle with a top
1 cup of aquarium gravel
stopwatch

1 cup of aquarium sand
blue food coloring

What to do . . .

❶. Add the sand and gravel to the empty bottle and then fill it about 3/4 full of water. Dye the water blue and put the cap on the bottle.

❷. Turn the bottle upside down and then right side up. Let the sand and gravel settle to the bottom. Use a stopwatch to time how long they take to settle.

❸. Which settles to the bottom first? Make a drawing to show this.

❹. Now repeat the activity. What happens?

Challenge

Imagine that you are a geologist who discovers a cliff that is made up of layers of rocks with fossils. Which layers do you think would have the oldest fossils? the youngest?

From the ExploraCenter Activity Booklet. Copyright © 1993 Scott, Foresman and Company.

43   Grade 4

---

gravel are shifted out of their resting position by powerful currents or by earth movements far below the surface. Since the rocks accumulate slowly, the bodies of many dead animals are covered by the sediment. When a fossil forms, minerals from the sediment replace minerals in the body.

Extensions and Experiments

Display some sedimentary rocks and have students use a magnifying lens to study the particles. If you have a rock with layers, students

may detect some differences in the size of the rock particles.

You may wish to have students repeat the activity using soil samples from various places instead of the

sand and gravel. They can make hypotheses about which materials will settle first.

DIFFICULTY LEVEL
AVERAGE
EASY   CHALLENGING

TIME NEEDED

30–40 MINUTES

Looking at Light

Is white light really white?

Materials you will need . . .

diffraction grating
white paper

desk lamp with unfrosted bulb or flashlight
colored pencils or crayons

What to do . . .

1. Switch on the desk lamp. Is the light white or pale yellow?

2. Now look at the light through the diffraction grating. Hold the diffraction grating up between a piece of white paper and the light. What do you see?

3. Use crayons or colored pencils to make a diagram showing the colors of light you see.

Challenge

If you are looking through a diffraction grating at light reflecting from the trees in a healthy rainforest, do you think the light will have a lot of green in it?

Activity 21

Teacher Notes

Science Process and Thinking Skills

observing*
interpreting data
predicting

Materials

- diffraction grating
- desk lamp with unfrosted bulb or flashlight
- white paper
- colored pencils or crayons

What to Expect

The students may have to move farther away from or closer to the light source depending on the strength of the bulb and background lighting conditions in the room. It would be best to darken the room as much as possible for this activity.

By projecting the spectrum on a sheet of white paper, the students will be able to easily identify the colors included in white light (red, orange, yellow, green, blue, indigo, and violet).

Science Background

Light waves bend as they travel through a slit. This bending is called *diffraction.* A diffraction grating is composed of many parallel grooves cut into a plastic strip.

Pure white light is actually composed of the colors of the spectrum. When we look at an object, the color we see depends on what colors are absorbed and what colors are reflected. A green leaf appears green because it reflects green light and absorbs the other colors. If we study a green colored object with a spectrascope we would see a spectrum that would have very little green in it.

When we see a rainbow in the sky, the colors are produced when

Activity 21

Looking at Light
Is white light really white?

Materials you will need . . .

diffraction grating
white paper

desk lamp with unfrosted bulb or flashlight
colored pencils or crayons

What to do . . .

1. Switch on the desk lamp. Is the light white or pale yellow?

2. Now look at the light through the diffraction grating. Hold the diffraction grating up between a piece of white paper and the light. What do you see?

3. Use crayons or colored pencils to make a diagram showing the colors of light you see.

Challenge

If you are looking through a diffraction grating at light reflecting from the trees in a healthy rainforest, do you think the light will have a lot of green in it?

From the Explora Center Activity Booklet. Copyright © 1993 Scott, Foresman and Company.

45   Grade 4

light bends from contact with drops of water in the air. The spectrum of colors is produced because the drops of water act like small prisms and break the white light from the sun into its colors.

Extensions and Experiments

Ask students to try the activity again, but this time they should try to think of a way to block certain colors.

DIFFICULTY LEVEL

AVERAGE

EASY   CHALLENGING

TIME NEEDED

20–30 MINUTES

Magnet Mix-up

What can a magnet move?

Materials you will need . . .

magnet
2 pennies
small foil pie plate

2 iron nails
2 soda cans

2 steel paper clips
paper plate

What to do . . .

1. Mix all the metal objects on the paper plate. Which objects do you think the magnet will move? Write down your guesses.

2. Drag the magnet over the mixture. What happens? Were you correct?

3. Can you think of a way to turn any of the objects into magnets themselves?

Challenge

Can you make a machine that will separate different kinds of metal? How many separate things might your machine do?

Science Process and Thinking Skills

classifying*
inferring

Materials

- magnet
- 2 iron nails
- 2 steel paper clips
- 2 pennies
- 2 soda cans
- paper plate
- small foil pie plate

What to Expect

🚫 Students should not bring magnets into contact with computer equipment.

The magnet will attract the nails and paper clips. The magnet will not attract non-ferrous metals, such as aluminum (soda can) and copper (penny).

Science Background

Magnets are objects that strongly attract iron or steel. A naturally occurring magnet is an iron ore called *magnetite,* commonly known as *lodestone.* It is possible to make artificial magnets by rubbing pieces of iron or steel with a magnet. Strong permanent magnets can be made by passing a powerful electric current near materials such as "alnico," a metal alloy made of aluminum, nickel, cobalt, and iron. Magnets that can be turned on and off are called *electromagnets.* They are made by placing a steel rod in a

core of electrical wires and passing current through the wires.

In industry, electromagnets are used more than permanent magnets especially when the magnets are used to move iron or steel objects.

You can imagine the problem of trying to move a steel object with a permanent magnet when it was time to put down the object that was picked up!

Magnet Mix-up

What can a magnet move?

Materials you will need . . .

magnet	2 iron nails	2 steel paper clips
2 pennies	2 soda cans	paper plate
small foil pie plate		

What to do . . .

❶. Mix all the metal objects on the paper plate. Which objects do you think the magnet will move? Write down your guesses.

❷. Drag the magnet over the mixture. What happens? Were you correct?

❸. Can you think of a way to turn any of the objects into magnets themselves?

Challenge

Can you make a machine that will separate different kinds of metal? How many separate things might your machine do?

47   Grade 4

Extensions and Experiments

Ask students to try to think of a way to show the presence of a magnetic field.

Possible Visual Response

① nails paperclips

② nails cans paperclips

48   Grade 4

DIFFICULTY LEVEL
AVERAGE
EASY   CHALLENGING

TIME NEEDED
15–20 MINUTES

Storm Warnings

How far away is lightning?

Materials you will need . . .

 stopwatch
paper
pencil

What to do . . .

1. When you see the sky light up from lightning, begin the stopwatch. Stop the stopwatch when you hear the thunder.

2. If the difference in time between when you see lightning and hear thunder is two seconds, how far away was the lightning?

3. If the stopwatch reads four seconds, how far away was the lightning? Ask your teacher to show you the chart for the answer.

Challenge

Try to figure out why you see lightning before you hear thunder.

Science Process and Thinking Skills

inferring
recognizing space
relationships
predicting*

Materials

- stopwatch
- paper
- pencil

What to Expect

This indoor activity needs to be done during a storm. The number of seconds between seeing the lightning flash and hearing the thunder, divided by five, yields the distance from the observer in miles.

seconds	distance
0	< 1 mile
5	1 mile
10	2 miles
15	3 miles

Since sound travels at about 1100 feet per second (about 331 meters per second) in air that is 32 degrees Fahrenheit (0 degrees Celsius) and light travels so fast students can't measure it with a stopwatch, the sound will reach them after the light.

Science Background

Lightning is a enormous electrical spark that sometimes accompanies stormy weather. Lightning can jump from cloud to cloud, from cloud to the ground, and from the ground to a cloud. When a lightning strike occurs, a great deal of heat energy is released. This energy produces a sound wave that travels through the air. Since the speed of light is so fast (186,000 miles/sec-

ond, or about 300,000 km/second), light from a lightning strike seems to reach us as soon as it is produced. On the other hand, sound travels very slowly so the thunder clap takes a few seconds to reach us. The delay between the arrival of the lightning flash and the thunder clap indicates the relative distance we are from the lightning bolt. If we notice the delay getting shorter, we can be sure that the storm is moving in our direction.

Storm Warnings
How far away is lightning?

Materials you will need . . .

stopwatch
paper
pencil

What to do . . .

1. When you see the sky light up from lightning, begin the stopwatch. Stop the stopwatch when you hear the thunder.

3. If the stopwatch reads four seconds, how far away was the lightning? Ask your teacher to show you the chart for the answer.

Challenge

Try to figure out why you see lightning before you hear thunder.

2. If the difference in time between when you see lightning and hear thunder is two seconds, how far away was the lightning?

From the *ExploraCenter Activity Booklet.* Copyright © 1993 Scott, Foresman and Company.

Extensions and Experiments

You can review safety rules that children should follow during a lightning storm.

DIFFICULTY LEVEL
AVERAGE

EASY CHALLENGING

TIME NEEDED

1 HOUR

From the *ExploraCenter Activity Booklet.* Copyright © 1993 Scott, Foresman and Company.

Which Way Is the Wind Blowing?

Can you build a wind vane?

Materials you will need . . .

plastic drinking straw	pencil with eraser	straight pin
index card	red marker	glue
scissors		

What to do . . .

1. Cut a slit in one end of your straw. Place the index card—straight up and down—in the slit and glue it into place. Find the balancing point of the straw by sliding it along your finger.

2. Push a pin through the straw, at the balancing point, into the pencil eraser. The wind vane should easily spin. Color the end of the straw red. This red area will point in the direction from which the wind is coming.

3. Go outside. Look at your wind vane. Which way does it say the wind is blowing? Now look at the trees. Which way are they moving?

4. Now move your wind vane to other areas around your school. What happens?

Challenge

Figure out how the wind blows around your school by taking readings at all of the corners of your building.

Activity 24

Teacher Notes

Science Process and Thinking Skills

observing
experimenting*
predicting

Materials

- plastic drinking straw
- pencil with eraser
- straight pin
- index card
- red marker
- glue
- scissors

What to Expect

Some students may be impatient and try to use the wind vane before the glue dries, so have the students wait for a few minutes after they apply the glue. While the glue dries, you can ask the class what kinds of wind vanes they've seen. You could also review the difference between north, south, east, and west.

Students will try to figure out in which direction the wind is blowing. The red end of the straw will point toward the origin of the wind.

Science Background

The weather in your region is greatly affected by the direction of the prevailing winds. If the wind is from the west, you are likely to experience the type of weather that occurred west of you. It is important to keep in mind that a wind vane points in the direction that the wind is *coming from* because the wind blows against the surface of the wind vane tail and pushes it away.

There are places on earth that have very little wind. One such place is an area called the "horse latitudes." The "horse latitudes" are 30 degrees north and south latitude. They are called the *horse latitudes*

Activity 24

Which Way Is the Wind Blowing?
Can you build a wind vane?

Materials you will need . . .

plastic drinking straw	pencil with eraser	straight pin
index card	red marker	glue
scissors		

What to do . . .

1. Cut a slit in one end of your straw. Place the index card—straight up and down—in the slit and glue it into place. Find the balancing point of the straw by sliding it along your finger.

2. Push a pin through the straw, at the balancing point, into the pencil eraser. The wind vane should easily spin. Color the end of the straw red. This red area will point in the direction from which the wind is coming.

3. Go outside. Look at your wind vane. Which way does it say the wind is blowing? Now look at the trees. Which way are they moving?

4. Now move your wind vane to other areas around your school. What happens?

Challenge

Figure out how the wind blows around your school by taking readings at all of the corners of your building.

51   Grade 4

---

because winds occur so seldom that sailing ships many years ago did not move significant distances for weeks and the horses on board had to be thrown overboard because there was insufficient food for them.

Extensions and Experiments

You can display a recent national weather map in your class. Have students study the map to see how wind direction and speed are noted. Can students use the map to figure out local conditions?

DIFFICULTY LEVEL

AVERAGE
EASY   CHALLENGING

TIME NEEDED
2 HOURS

Water Saver

How much water do you waste?

Materials you will need . . .

stopwatch
8 ounce paper cup
water fountain

What to do . . .

1. When you drink from a fountain, how many many cups of water do you think go down the drain? How many cups do you think go down the drain each day?

2. Now go to the water fountain with your cup and stopwatch. Turn on the fountain and ask a friend to time how long it takes to fill the paper cup. How much water comes out of the fountain each second?

3. Now have two friends take a drink from the fountain. Time how long the fountain is on before they put their mouths to it and how long they leave the fountain on after they have finished.

4. Can you think of a way to figure out how much water is wasted each day?

Challenge

Where does your community get water? How is the water treated to make it safe to drink?

Science Process and Thinking Skills

measuring*
communicating

Materials

- stopwatch
- 8 ounce paper cup
- water fountain

What to Expect

In this activity, students will determine how much water is wasted each time a person takes a drink from a fountain. They will also estimate how much water is wasted at a fountain in a day.

For this activity, students will have to leave the room to measure water use at a drinking fountain. If students watch the fountain, they can see how often it is used. For example, they will see whether students pass the fountain when they return from recess or lunch.

To guess how much water is wasted, students need to determine how much water is used per second and how many people use the fountain each day.

Science Background

The importance of this activity relates very directly to the larger question of water conservation in a community. Preserving supplies of fresh clean water is a critical problem for many communities. Our individual behavior often leads to wasting this precious resource.

Most humans are used to having water always available for drinking. Animals don't have regular access to water, so they drink anywhere and anytime they can find it. Camels can drink about 30 gallons of water at a time and can live for about ten days without it.

Water Saver
How much water do you waste?

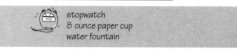

Materials you will need . . .

stopwatch
8 ounce paper cup
water fountain

What to do . . .

❶. When you drink from a fountain, how many many cups of water do you think go down the drain? How many cups do you think go down the drain each day?

❷. Now go to the water fountain with your cup and stopwatch. Turn on the fountain and ask a friend to time how long it takes to fill the paper cup. How much water comes out of the fountain each second?

❸. Now have two friends take a drink from the fountain. Time how long the fountain is on before they put their mouths to it and how long they leave the fountain on after they have finished.

❹. Can you think of a way to figure out how much water is wasted each day?

Challenge

Where does your community get water? How is the water treated to make it safe to drink?

Extensions and Experiments

You may choose to make a strong connection to language arts, social studies, and art by encouraging the students to start a campaign for water conservation at the school. They can display of posters showing the results of their work and suggest ways to conserve water.

DIFFICULTY LEVEL

AVERAGE

EASY   CHALLENGING

TIME NEEDED

2 HOURS

Matter in Motion

Can you see currents?

Materials you will need . . .

Ivory™ liquid
2 liter plastic bottle
funnel

water
large plastic bowl

food coloring
small cup

What to do . . .

❶. Gently pour some soap and water (one part soap to twenty parts water) into the bowl. Don't shake it.

❷. Add a few drops of food coloring to the mixture. Use the funnel to put it in the plastic bottle.

❸. Put the bottle in a well lit place. Do you see patterns in the water? Are there dark or light patches?

❹. Now gently swirl the bottle so the mixture starts to turn. Have the patterns changed? What might cause these changes?

Challenge

Can you see currents in a pie plate? If not, how can you create them?

Science Process and Thinking Skills

observing
making a hypothesis*
making and using models

Materials

* Ivory™ liquid
* water
* food coloring
* 2 liter plastic bottle
* small cup
* large plastic bowl
* funnel

What to Expect

🚫 If you have a sink, ask students to do their pouring over it.

The food coloring will show a darker tint in the areas where the soap is more concentrated. Ask students not to mix the soap and water too vigorously to avoid mixing it into the water. The students will be able to see the patterns in the liquid change as the bottle is gently swirled.

Science Background

This activity is roughly analogous to the affect of the moving surface of a planet under its atmosphere—the parts of the atmosphere closest to the planet surface are disturbed by the planet's motion.

Heat energy from the sun travels through a planetary atmosphere and is partly absorbed by it. On Earth, much of the heat energy gets through the atmosphere and heats our planet's surface. In time, this heat warms the atmosphere above the ground and water. As the heated atmosphere rises, cooler air flows down to replace it. This type of air movement is called a *convection current*.

Activity
26

Matter in Motion
Can you see currents?

Materials you will need . . .

Ivory™ liquid
2 liter plastic bottle
funnel

water
large plastic bowl

food coloring
small cup

What to do . . .

1. Gently pour some soap and water (one part soap to twenty parts water) into the bowl. Don't shake it.

2. Add a few drops of food coloring to the mixture. Use the funnel to put it in the plastic bottle.

3. Put the bottle in a well lit place. Do you see patterns in the water? Are there dark or light patches?

4. Now gently swirl the bottle so the mixture starts to turn. Have the patterns changed? What might cause these changes?

Challenge

Can you see currents in a pie plate? If not, how can you create them?

55   Grade 4

The extent of convection current production depends on a variety of factors, including the composition of the atmosphere and how much energy the planet receives from the sun.

Extensions and Experiments

Ask students to find color photos of planetary atmospheres in books. Ask them to look for patterns that might be related to the heating and cooling.

You can demonstrate convection currents. Prepare some dark colored cold water and some light colored hot water. Fill a container halfway with the hot water. Then very

gently pour in the dark colored cold water. The students will see the darker water sink and observe some convection currents form.

DIFFICULTY LEVEL — AVERAGE — EASY — CHALLENGING

TIME NEEDED — 30–40 MINUTES

Sound Speed

Can you measure the speed of sound?

Materials you will need . . .

drum
drumstick
stopwatch

What to do . . .

1. Ask a friend to take the drum and drumstick and walk 10 steps away from you. Ask him or her to bang on the drum slowly 5 times. Do you hear anything?

2. Now have your friend walk 100 steps away. Watch and listen as he or she bangs on the drum slowly 5 times. Do you hear anything?

3. Now have your friend walk 500 steps away. Do you see the drumstick hit the drum and hear the sound at the same time?

4. Use the stopwatch to time how long it takes you to hear the sound. Time from the point when your friend beats the drum until you hear the sound.

Challenge

Can you create echoes by standing near a high wall and shouting? How?

Activity 27

Teacher Notes

DISCOVER THE WONDER

Module D

Science Process and Thinking Skills

measuring
inferring*

Materials

- drum
- drumstick
- stopwatch

What to Expect

The students will see that at great distances they can see the drum being hit before they hear the sound. To ensure that the sound reaches these distances, you might want to have two or three drums and drumsticks available. Ask the students with the instruments to go directly to the locations away from the observers. At a distance of 500 steps, the time between seeing and hearing will be observable.

Science Background

The speed of sound varies with temperature and the medium through which it passes. The speed of sound is about 331 meters per second in air that is 0 degrees Celsius. At 20 degrees Celsius, sound travels 342 meters per second.

The speed of light is 300,000 kilometers per second. It is much faster than sound, does not vary with temperature, and does not require a medium.

Light reaches our eyes before sound reaches our ears. Imagine for a moment that it takes half a second for you to respond to seeing a drum being hit 330 meters away and one second to respond to hearing a sound. Any measurements about the actual difference between the arrival of the sound waves and light waves is affected by reaction time.

Since light travels so fast it has often been used as a way for people

---

Activity 27

Sound Speed
Can you measure the speed of sound?

Materials you will need . . .

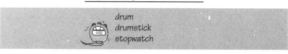

drum
drumstick
stopwatch

What to do . . .

1. Ask a friend to take the drum and drumstick and walk 10 steps away from you. Ask him or her to bang on the drum slowly 5 times. Do you hear anything?

2. Now have your friend walk 100 steps away. Watch and listen as he or she bangs on the drum slowly 5 times. Do you hear anything?

3. Now have your friend walk 500 steps away. Do you see the drumstick hit the drum and hear the sound at the same time?

4. Use the stopwatch to time how long it takes you to hear the sound. Time from the point when your friend beats the drum until you hear the sound.

Challenge

Can you create echoes by standing near a high wall and shouting? How?

From the *ExploraCenter Activity Booklet.* Copyright © 1993 Scott, Foresman and Company.

57   **Grade 4**

---

to communicate. Ships can send messages to one another by flashing strong lights on and off in a code. Thousands of years ago, people could communicate over long distances by setting fires on mountain tops or towers.

Extensions and Experiments

From a great distance it will be difficult to see a drumstick hit a drum. Ask students to try to think of a way to solve this problem.

58   **Grade 4**

DIFFICULTY LEVEL

AVERAGE

EASY   CHALLENGING

TIME NEEDED

40–50 MINUTES

From the *ExploraCenter Activity Booklet.* Copyright © 1993 Scott, Foresman and Company.

Shake It, Don't Break It!

How are earthquakes caused?

Materials you will need . . .

dessert gelatin, cut in strips	flat plate
water	paper towels

What to do . . .

1. Wet the plate so the gelatin will slide easily. Take one of the gelatin strips, lay it on the plate, and push both ends together. What do you see at the middle of the strip?

2. Take one of the strips and hold it at each end. Gently pull on both ends. Be careful not to break the strip! What do you see now?

3. Now take one of the strips, lay in on a wet plate, and pull on each end. Keep pulling the ends until the strip breaks. What do you see?

Challenge

If you were a seismologist, what instruments would you use to measure the changes that happen when rock layers move and break?

Science Process and Thinking Skills

predicting*
inferring

Materials

- 4 boxes of dessert gelatin
- flat plate
- water
- paper towels

What to Expect

Follow the instructions for preparing one batch of dessert gelatin but instead of adding one box of gelatin, add four. Pour the liquid in a rectangular pan to set. After it sets, cut the gelatin into strips 15 cm long and 2 cm wide. Make sure the gelatin is very firm. After cutting the strips, immerse the bottom of the container in warm water for a few minutes to loosen the gelatin.

When the students work on pulling the ends of their "rock layers," they may find them slippery. They can use paper towels to improve their grip.

Science Background

Heat energy within the earth and the movement of the crustal plates apply enormous pressure to rock layers. When rock layers are pushed, they sometimes bulge or sink. Occasionally, the pressure is strong enough to actually break the layers. These breaks are called *geologic faults.* If the fault is large and a lot of energy is released in the process, we can sense the earth moving.

The movement in the earth's surface is also caused by a downward push from the weight of new material that deposits on top of older material. For example, over a period of many years, the Mississippi River has carried an enormous amount of

---

Shake It, Don't Break It!
How are earthquakes caused?

Materials you will need . . .

| dessert gelatin, cut in strips | flat plate |
| water | paper towels |

What to do . . .

1. Wet the plate so the gelatin will slide easily. Take one of the gelatin strips, lay it on the plate, and push both ends together. What do you see at the middle of the strip?

3. Now take one of the strips, lay in on a wet plate, and pull on each end. Keep pulling the ends until the strip breaks. What do you see?

Challenge

If you were a seismologist, what instruments would you use to measure the changes that happen when rock layers move and break?

2. Take one of the strips and hold it at each end. Gently pull on both ends. Be careful not to break the strip! What do you see now?

59   Grade 4

---

sand and mud into the Gulf of Mexico. As a result, the earth's crust under the Gulf of Mexico has been pushed down. The water

hasn't deepened because the sediment that has been deposited raises the actual level of the floor of the Gulf of Mexico.

Extensions and Experiments

Have the students do research into the various kinds of faults that occur when rock layers fracture. They can use gelatin strips to represent these faults.

Ask students to find out more about faults. Thrust faults occur when one layer moves over another, and normal faults occur when the layers just move up and down.

DIFFICULTY LEVEL

AVERAGE

EASY   CHALLENGING

TIME NEEDED

20–30 MINUTES

Light Benders
Can mirrors capture the sun's energy?

Materials you will need . . .

reflective paper

What to do . . .

1. Hold the reflective paper an arm's length away. Bend it slightly so it bends outward toward you. Can you see your face? Is it right side up or upside down?

2. Now hold the reflective paper so the center is pushed away from you. Raise one hand. Can you see an image form? If you can't, move the reflective paper back and forth until you can.

3. Make a drawing that shows how you think a light ray bouncing off your face travels as it hits the reflective paper.

Challenge

Can you design a solar collector that can cook a hot dog? Make a drawing that shows how your solar collector would work. Then test it!

Science Process and Thinking Skills

observing
experimenting*

Materials

• reflective paper

What to Expect

Students should not fold or crease the reflective paper.

In this activity, students discover that if a flexible mirror is formed into a concave shape (the center is pushed away from the observer) an inverted image forms. This image forms because the mirror brings light into a focus in front of it. The image is called a *real image* and in fact lies somewhat closer to the observer than the focal point of the mirror.

Science Background

The outer part of the sun that we see from Earth is called the *photosphere*. It gives off the light we receive. Now and then scientists have observed disturbances called *sunspots* on the photosphere. These areas give off less heat than the rest of the sun and appear to move across the photosphere. When there is a lot of sunspot activity, radio and television broadcasts on Earth are disturbed.

A great deal of energy reaches the Earth's surface from the sun. Green plants capture some of it, but most of the energy is absorbed by the earth or reflected out into the atmosphere.

Light and heat reaching a concave mirror is brought to a focus in front of the mirror and can be used to raise the temperature of any object placed at the mirror's focal

---

Light Benders

Can mirrors capture the sun's energy?

Materials you will need . . .

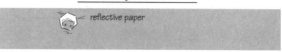

reflective paper

What to do . . .

❶. Hold the reflective paper an arm's length away. Bend it slightly so it bends outward toward you. Can you see your face? Is it right side up or upside down?

❷. Now hold the reflective paper so the center is pushed away from you. Raise one hand. Can you see an image form? If you can't, move the reflective paper back and forth until you can.

❸. Make a drawing that shows how you think a light ray bouncing off your face travels as it hits the reflective paper.

Challenge

Can you design a solar collector that can cook a hot dog? Make a drawing that shows how your solar collector would work. Then test it!

From the *ExploraCenter Activity Booklet.* Copyright © 1993 Scott, Foresman and Company.

61   Grade 4

---

point. In commercial applications of solar collectors, this heat is converted into electrical energy. A *solar collector* is any device that can be used to capture the sun's energy and transform it into some useful form.

Extensions and Experiments

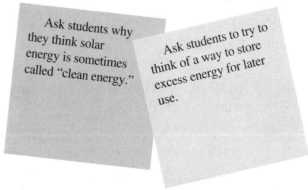

Ask students why they think solar energy is sometimes called "clean energy."

Ask students to try to think of a way to store excess energy for later use.

DIFFICULTY LEVEL

AVERAGE

EASY   CHALLENGING

TIME NEEDED

30–40 MINUTES

From the *ExploraCenter Activity Booklet.* Copyright © 1993 Scott, Foresman and Company.

Keep Warm! Stay Cool!

Is air a good insulator?

Materials you will need . . .

thermal card
stopwatch
small and large sealable plastic bags

desk
sunny window

What to do . . .

1. What color is the thermal card? Put the thermal card in a sunny window. What color is it now?

2. Now put it under a desk and use the stopwatch to time how long it takes to change back to its original color.

3. Repeat Steps 1 and 2, but after you warm the card, place it in a plastic bag. Seal the bag and put it under a desk. Time how long it takes for the card to change color.

4. Heat the card again, put it in a small bag, and seal it. Then put the smaller bag in a larger bag. Place the larger bag under a desk. How long does it take for the card to change color?

Challenge

Design a coat that you can wear in the cold weather. Use some ideas from this activity and make sure the coat uses air as an insulator.

DISCOVER THE WONDER

Module E

Science Process and Thinking Skills

inferring*
experimenting

Materials

- thermal card
- stopwatch
- small and large sealable plastic bags
- desk
- sunny window

What to Expect

The students will see that as they increase the number of layers of air held around the thermal card they will increase the amount of time it takes for the card to heat and cool.

Science Background

The best insulator for heat energy is a vacuum since there are very few molecules of gas within it that can conduct energy. Air works as a surprisingly effective insulator because it has relatively few molecules per unit of volume when compared to a solid. To create an effective insulating material for clothing, manufacturers design garments that trap a lot of air. Down parkas work effectively because the small feathers contained within the material trap the air.

The importance of understanding insulators extends to the study of energy conservation. If you live in a very hot climate, you are aware that buildings must be well insulated to reduce the flow of heat energy into the building, particularly if the building is air conditioned. In a colder climate, insulation reduces the flow of heat energy out of a building. One of nature's most surprising insulators is snow. Native North Americans learned long ago that building a house out of snow (an

Keep Warm! Stay Cool!

Is air a good insulator?

Materials you will need . . .

 thermal card   desk
stopwatch   sunny window
small and large sealable plastic bags

What to do . . .

1. What color is the thermal card? Put the thermal card in a sunny window. What color is it now?

2. Now put it under a desk and use the stopwatch to time how long it takes to change back to its original color.

3. Repeat Steps 1 and 2, but after you warm the card, place it in a plastic bag. Seal the bag and put it under a desk. Time how long it takes for the card to change color.

4. Heat the card again, put it in a small bag, and seal it. Then put the smaller bag in a larger bag. Place the larger bag under a desk. How long does it take for the card to change color?

Challenge

Design a coat that you can wear in the cold weather. Use some ideas from this activity and make sure the coat uses air as an insulator.

igloo) could protect them from very cold outside temperatures. The snow blocks used in igloo construction contain lots of trapped air that acts as an insulator. A small fire built inside an igloo can make the inside temperature high enough to make a person perspire.

Extensions and Experiments

Ask students to think of ways to keep an ice cube from melting, if it is exposed to warm air.

DIFFICULTY LEVEL

AVERAGE

EASY   CHALLENGING

TIME NEEDED

40–50 MINUTES

Appendix

Teachers' Guide to the Explorabook

by Anne Hayes and the Exploratorium Staff

Welcome to the ExploraCenter. Included is the *Explorabook,* a printed version of the Exploratorium museum. Founded in 1969, and located in San Francisco, California, the Exploratorium is a one-of-a-kind science museum dedicated to discovery. The Exploratorium has more than 600 interactive exhibits that visitors are encouraged to poke, toss, squeeze, and squint at, press, listen to, and look through.

About the Exploratorium

Each year, 600,000 people visit the museum; more than 60,000 of them are students, brought by teachers from around the San Francisco Bay Area. From the very beginning, these teachers asked the Exploratorium to help bring the museum's way of teaching science into their classrooms and make learning science more fun for student and teacher alike. In response, the Exploratorium created two teacher-training programs: the School in the Exploratorium for elementary-school teachers and the Teacher Institute for middle- and high-school teachers.

While local students are off for the summer, some of their teachers are at the Exploratorium, playing with exhibits and experimenting in our classroom. By taking the time to explore, teachers rediscover their own joy in learning. Through their own discoveries, they develop new ways to teach science. The Exploratorium's teacher programs are highly successful, and the museum is recognized by educators nationwide as a standard-bearer in teaching hands-on science. The museum's educational programs are supported by grants from groups, such as the National Science Foundation, the United States Department of Education, and the California Department of Education. About 2,000 teachers have participated in the elementary school program since it began almost twenty years ago. In the eight and a half years since the Teacher Institute was founded, it has trained about 900 middle- and high-school teachers. (For more information about Exploratorium programs, write to the Center for Teaching and Learning at 3601 Lyon Street, San Francisco, CA 94123.)

About the *Explorabook*

The *Explorabook* comes out of this playful learning environment. Nearly three years in the making, the *Explorabook* was first published in the fall of 1991. The book was an immediate success. Praised in reviews, Explorabook was named Nonfiction Children's Book of the Year by *Publisher's Weekly.*

The author of the *Explorabook* is John Cassidy, president of Klutz Press. Cassidy has published twenty other Klutz books, all of which share the same let's-have-fun attitude. Working with the Exploratorium staff, John conceived the *Explorabook* as a mini-Exploratorium, a series of flattened exhibits for children to pick up and bring to life.

The experiments and activities in the *Explorabook* are designed not only to demonstrate principles, but to teach an approach and a process. The approach is one of creativity and open-mindedness; the process is scientific.

Science, the Art of Discovery

In the final chapter of the *Explorabook*, readers learn that the human brain sometimes glosses over things, jumping to conclusions and making assumptions. In our daily lives, it's impossible not to do this.

You know the route to work, for example. You don't need to reconsider it each day. Yet even on that route, it's delightful to be startled by something you have never noticed before: perhaps a handsome tree at the corner where you turn left or a new restaurant within walking distance of the

school. In that moment of noticing you are opening your mind and beginning to discover. Openness is where science begins. The scientist cultivates it and brings it to bear on whatever interests him or her.

Consider Isaac Newton, for example. You might know him best for his interest in gravity and mechanical forces. But Newton also brought an open mind to the study of optics and made many important discoveries in that field.

In the 1670s, when Newton was experimenting, people believed that the cascade of colors you see when light passes through a prism was the result of the glass itself, not the light shining through it. Newton, however, questioned this idea. Perhaps he noticed the similarity between the pattern of colors cast by a prism and the colors of a rainbow and wondered how such similar effects could have such different origins. Or perhaps he noticed the way a spectrum appears and disappears, depending upon the way the prism is held. We can't be sure what Newton noticed, but we don't have to be; what is important is knowing that he was noticing, because being open means noticing things.

Newton did more than just notice. Taking a prism, he held it in a beam of sunlight and cast a rainbow against the opposite wall. Then he pulled the curtain to allow a single shaft of light into the room. By narrowing his light source, he created a well defined spectrum with which he could experiment with more easily. Newton reasoned that if the glass was creating the colors, then passing the colors through more glass should make no difference. To test this, he got

EUREKA!

another prism, and held it in the path of the colors created by the first. Instead of seeing the second prism cast the same colors, Newton watched a narrow band of white light appear on the wall where the spectrum had previously been!

Picture Newton toying with the second prism, moving it in and out of the path of the spectrum, shifting its faces, looking for another band of color, or white light. This kind of activity lies at the heart of science. To test something patiently, curiously, to try the same step over again, and then to try a new one, is to engage in science. You don't learn to play the piano just by looking at the keys. In science, as in art, you learn by doing.

Doing Science

The best way to understand what Newton was doing is to do the same thing yourself. But maybe you haven't got a prism. For a try at practicing science, take a look at the Fresnel lens in the *Explorabook* instead.

What do you notice about the lens? Nothing is too obvious. You might notice it is clear. It is smooth on one side and has ridges on the other. You can look through it. When you do, things look bigger than they really are. They look bigger and either fuzzier or very clear.

Turn to the chapter called "Bending Light

Waves," beginning on page 18 of the *Explorabook*. The activities illustrates one of the properties of the lens, so they'll help you continue to test and probe. The first activity, "Weird Faces," introduces you to magnification; the second, "TV for Bats," teaches about making images; and the third, "Nuclear-Cooked Hot Dog," shows how to focus sunlight with the lens.

As you proceed, you'll probably be tempted to look for explanations. Why did my partner's eye get so big? What's happening when I cook the hot dog? When you want to know why, try asking "What if..." instead. Understanding grows out of what you notice. Rather than immediately searching for an explanation, search for ways to notice even more.

Being open and noticing are just the beginning of doing science. To further enrich your perceptions and to begin to understand them better, we suggest the following steps:

- **Record what you see.**

    For example, review the steps you took to do the "Weird Faces" activity in the *Explorabook* and write them out:

    "The lens is in front of my friend's face, as close as possible."

    "I stand ten steps back."

    "My friend moves the lens away from her face: at half her arm's length, I see the huge eye."

- **Make measurements.**

    You've already done this in the notes above. "Ten steps" and "Half an arm's length" are measures of distance.

- **Find a way to make the same thing happen again.**

    Make something else huge, like the eyeball in "Weird Faces." Or use the lens to turn something else upside down.

From the *ExploraCenter Activity Booklet*. Copyright © 1993 Scott, Foresman and Company.

- **Look for other things that do what the lens does.**

   Have you ever noticed that a water drop makes whatever it sits on look bigger? Or that waves on the surface of a swimming pool focus light into bright, shifting lines on the bottom of the pool?

- **Compare similar effects.**

   When you look at your reflection in a spoon, it is upside down, just as your image was in "TV for Bats." What do a spoon and a lens have in common? Can you duplicate the Fresnel lens activities with the lens of a magnifying glass?

- **Categorize your observations.**

   You've noticed that the lens makes things bigger, so you could make "magnification" your first category. List all the things you've found that can magnify something else. Think up other categories.

- **Focus on one detail and change it.**

   When you did "TV for Bats," for instance, you turned off the lights. What happens when you turn them back on? Turn the lights off again, and try making an image with other objects besides the TV—hold the lens up to a radio, a window, a lamp. Then try these things with the light on again. What differences do you notice?

- **Guess at explanations.**

   Based on what you just did—turning the overhead light on and off—you can guess something about how a lens works. It makes images using the light from an object. The stronger the ambient light, the more difficult it is to see the image made by light coming from an object.

- **Test your guesses.**

   If you've got a three-way light bulb, compare the image the lens makes at the three different settings. Is the highest setting the easiest image to see?

Discovery in the Classroom

The procedures you've just practiced can be applied to all the experiments and activities in the *Explorabook* and the ExploraCenter. But you may be wondering how to "apply" the *Explorabook* itself specifically to your classroom. How can you "assign" it to your students?

First, consider simply leaving the book lying around the classroom and letting the children find it when they will. One local teacher keeps a Fresnel lens like the ones in the *Explorabook* and ExploraCenter hanging from the ceiling of his classroom all the time. He says "Exciting science

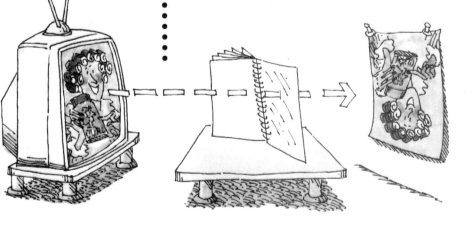

materials do not always have to tie directly into the curriculum. Interesting materials that engage students interest and trigger their questions are important."

Chances are you'll want to bring the *Explorabook* into the classroom more directly. Plan on having students work in groups of four to six. We have found that groups of students working together generate ideas. The students play off of each other's ideas and learn more together than one student would alone. Each student will have the chance to find and use his or her strengths, and all will develop problem-solving skills. Along with the excitement that builds as students discover science, another kind of excitement develops as the students discover a new way to be with each other.

Let each group choose which activities to do. Allowing the students to choose is like leaving the book around for them to pick up: it engages them. Make sure each group chooses different activities, so that each can explain their project to the others. The students will do plenty of talking as they work together, but requiring them to present their work to the other groups provides you with a means to evaluate their work (as it proceeds, and

at its conclusion), as well as giving the students an important impetus to understand what they're doing.

As the students work, introduce them to the procedures you tried out in the previous section of the guide. Tell them to write down everything they notice. Ask them what else they can think of that does the same thing as a lens, a magnet, or a diffraction grating. Then help them compare these similar things. Show them how to make simple measurements. Help them compare and categorize their findings. Encourage them to guess at explanations and to test their guesses.

As work progresses, you can expect questions. When students ask "Why?" help them turn that into "What if...." Remind them of the steps in the "Doing Science" section. Tell them asking more questions is the best way to find an explanation.

You can also expect that something will go wrong at some point. You won't get the results you expect, or something will happen that you just can't figure out. When that moment comes, tell your kids that trial and error is part of the scientific process, and ask them to suggest what else you can try. Approach the obstacle openly and creatively, and you'll find your way around it.

Once the students are familiar with the activities, you can suggest they build exhibits from them, in true Exploratorium style. Use two binder clips, for instance, to stand the Fresnel lens on a table top. Using the *Explorabook* and their own notes, your kids can write instructions that other students can follow as they experiment with the lens. Then help them write an explanation of the lens's effects. You can adapt all of the *Explorabook* and Explora-Center activities in this way, and eventually you can build a

From the *ExploraCenter Activity Booklet.* Copyright © 1993 Scott, Foresman and Company.

science museum from all the exhibits. Or instead of a creating a museum, your class could write their own book of science activities based on their discoveries.

At the Exploratorium, ESL and Special Education teachers have had particular success with activities like those in the *Explorabook* and ExploraCenter. The enjoyable activities these resources provide motivate learning in all areas, not just in science.

Going Further

You can begin your exploration of science by experimenting with the tools and activities in the *Explorabook* and the ExploraCenter. To expand your experimentation, you may need more tools. You can order additional copies of the tools in the *Explorabook* from the Exploratorium Store at 1-800-359-9899.

The *Explorabook* and ExploraCenter provide many activities for your classroom. If you would like to create your own activities, the teachers at the Exploratorium offer these suggestions for going further.

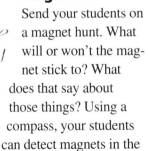

Magnetism

Send your students on a magnet hunt. What will or won't the magnet stick to? What does that say about those things? Using a compass, your students can detect magnets in the classroom and in their homes. (If you don't have a compass, make one using the directions in the *Explorabook*.) The magnetic compass needle will respond to the presence of other magnets. You'll find magnets where you might not expect them. Many motors, for example, will attract the needle of a compass.

Bending Light Waves

To see the path that the light follows as it passes through the lens, clap a couple of chalkboard erasers together to fill the air with dust and shine a thin beam of light through the lens. (You can use light from a flashlight or a laser.) The dust makes the beam visible. What happens to the beam as it passes through the lens?

Bacterial Stories

Even if you run out of agar, you can grow bacteria on slices of raw potato. We recommend that you seal each potato slice (or agar dish) in a plastic sealable bag. When you are done, throw the bag away without opening it, keeping the bacteria sealed away from your students.

Light Wave Craziness

A diffraction grating bends light to create color. You can duplicate this effect with a tea strainer, a black umbrella, a silk scarf, or a nylon stocking. Set up a small bright light and look at it through the tea strainer, the taut cloth of the umbrella, the fabric of the scarf or nylon stocking. Compare the views through different cloths and screens.

Homemade Science

Try balancing a ping pong ball in the flow of air from a hair dryer. Experiment with changing the air flow—making it slower or faster. Can you balance two balloons in the air flow? Tie strings to the balloons and hang the balloons so that they are about a foot apart. Direct the air flow so that it passes between the balloons. What happens to the balloons?

Bouncing Light Rays

With several small mirrors, you can construct a mirror maze. Prop a mirror up so that it is perpendicular to the floor. Shine a flashlight beam so that it grazes the floor and reflects from the mirror. Adjust the mirror so that the reflected beam also grazes the floor. Set up another mirror so that it reflects the reflected beam. Can you make the reflected beams go where you want them to go, following a complex path across your classroom?

Optical Illusions

Moiré patterns, like the ones that you see in the moiré spinner on the front of the *Explorabook*, appear when you superimpose two patterns of closely spaced lines and move one set of lines. Use two combs to create your own moiré patterns. Hold the combs parallel to each other so that the teeth are superimposed. Move one comb and watch for the moving moiré patterns.

Additional Resources

Once you've taken hold of hands-on science and want to run with it, look for these publications to help you.

Publications from the Exploratorium:

Order by calling the Exploratorium Store at 1-800-359-9899.

Exploring Magazine, $18 per year; published quarterly.

Each issue focuses on a single topic; past topics include electricity, illusions, and dirt. Though the magazine is written for a general audience, each issue contains at least one activity related to the magazine's theme. Information from many articles can be integrated into classroom lessons.

Exploratorium Science Snackbook, $25

Over 100 classroom science projects written by teachers, for teachers. Each project is based on an exhibit at the Exploratorium. Projects are geared for grades 6 to 12, but most are adaptable to any age group.

Other Publications:

Available in many book stores.

Ball-Point Pens: A Children's Museum Activity Book, by Bernie Zubrowski. Little, Brown and Co., 1979.
Bubbles: A Children's Museum Activity Book, by Bernie Zubrowski. Little, Brown and Co., 1979.

Both of the above titles are part of a series put together by the Boston Children's Museum. The series contains books on many different science topics by different authors and publishers.

From the *ExploraCenter Activity Booklet.* Copyright © 1993 Scott, Foresman and Company.

Gee Whiz! by Linda Allison and David Katz. Little, Brown, 1983. One of the Brown Paper School Book series, which offers many creative, science-oriented activities.

GEMS, by Lawrence Hall of Science, University of California,, Berkeley, CA 94720. A series of activity-based publications covering everything from bubbles to fingerprinting.

Ontario Science Center Activity Books. Addison Wesley. A series of activity books for younger children. Titles include *Sportworks, Foodworks,* and *Scienceworks.*

The Way Things Work, by David Macaulay. Houghton Mifflin, 1988. A good reference work for basic scientific principles. Illustrates how many, many machines work, from flush toilets to compact disc players.

TOPS Learning Systems, 10970 Mulino Rd., Canby, OR 97013. Activity cards for physical science projects using everyday materials. Content is very wide ranging.

Science Resources

Professional Organizations

There are many organizations that support science education at the elementary level. Listed below are several resources and organizations you can depend on for support, curriculum ideas, continuing education, and professional fulfillment.

American Association for the Advancement of Science (AAAS)
1333 H St., N.W.
Washington, DC 20005
202-326-6400

National Science Supervisors Association (NSSA)
c/o Robert Foriel
P. O. Box AL
Amagancett, NY 11930

National Science Teacher's Association (NSTA)
1742 Connecticut Avenue, N.W.
Washington, DC 20009

Science Teacher Education Journal
Leila Lee
John Wiley and Sons, Inc.
605 3rd Avenue
New York, NY 10158

Funding Sources

There are many local or regional resources available to you.

Local and State Departments of National Resources and Recreation
They usually have resource material, curriculum material, and experts that can assist you in class planning.

District or County Superintendent's Office
Most offices have a Science Curriculum Specialist or Coordinator available to the teachers within that district or county. They are a valuable resource for science activities, funding and procurement for materials, and professional support.

Local Zoos, Museums, and Aquariums
Many have education departments and programs already in place for your support. Some even offer programming that they will bring into your classroom. The staffs of these institutions are glad to assist you in developing science curricula and programs for your classroom.

Local Businesses
Pet shops, architecture and engineering firms, and a host of other local resources can aid in your science instruction. The professionals who manage and staff these businesses are usually more than willing to contribute some of their time and expertise to you and your classroom. It provides positive exposure for their business. They can aid you with materials, livestock, and technical sup-

port. Depending on the ability and willingness of the professional, you may even be able to utilize them to present a science topic to your class.

By using the local and regional resources that are available to you, you can enrich your classroom presentations, provide more relevant applications of science for your students, and take some of the load off your shoulders.

Stores

School Supply Stores

Most communities have one or more school supply stores that will carry the majority of the materials required in these experiments. Consult the Yellow Pages under "School Supplies—Retail" or some similar heading. Then check with one or more of them. You might find a great source of educational resources right in your own backyard.

Catalogs

Check with your school office for educational supply catalogs. Numerous catalogers probably mail to your school. Find out where these are filed. They, too, will carry most, if not all, of the materials required in these activities and can prove to be exceptional resources for you in your teaching.

Hardware Stores

Several of the materials required may also be available in your local hardware store, which routinely carry plaster of Paris, clear empty containers, small cups, etc.

Science Museum Stores

Any number of good science museums have a wealth of resources that savvy teachers already tap into. If none are available in your immediate area, try contacting:

The Exploratorium Store

3601 Lyon Street
San Francisco, CA 94123
Write for a catalog, or phone 1-800-359-9899.

Scientific Supply Companies

Several companies make a specialty of supplying scientific materials. Below is a partial listing of some of the better known ones.

Sargent-Welch Scientific Company

7300 N. Linder Ave.
Skokie, IL 60077
1-800-SARGENT

Carolina Biological Supply, Co.

2700 York Road
Burlington, NC 27215
1-800-334-5551

Delta Education

P.O. Box 950
Hudson, NH 90068
1-800-442-5444

Edmund Scientific

101 E. Glouster Pike
Barrington, NJ 08007

Frey Scientific Co.

905 Hickory Lane
Mansfield, OH 44905

Fisher Scientific Company

4901 W. LeMoyne St.
Chicago, IL 60651

Science Kit & Boreal Laboratories

777 E. Bark Drive
Tonawanda, NY 14150
1-800-828-7777

For magnets:

Dowling Magnets

P.O. Box 1829
Sonoma, CA 95476
707-935-0352

For more reflective paper, stopwatches, thermal cards, etc.:

Replacement sets of tools are available through ScottForesman (1-800-554-4411) for a nominal fee.

For replacements of a single tool or multiple copies of one tool, try either the Exploratorium Store (phone 1-800-359-9899) or one of the scientific supply companies.

Books

Teacher Resources

Creative Sciencing

Over 160 open-ended activities generate lots of
questions and
connections,
involving stu-
dents in the
process of scien-
tific inquiry.
Students explore,
discover, and
experiment in biology, chemistry, earth and environmental science, and physics.

320 pp. $18.95 (0-673-52008-0)   Gr K-6

The Complete Science Fair Handbook

Helps you plan and prepare a successful science fair, with project ideas, timetables, research
sources, and information on how projects are
judged. Plus
terrific ideas
and strategies
to stimulate stu-
dents' creativity
and to develop
their appreciation
of science.

96 pp. $8.95 (0-673-38800-X)   Gr 3-6

The Whole Cosmos Catalog of Science Activities

This giant-sized
volume of over 275
activities helps you
put more wonder and
excitement into a
child's science back-
round. There are
easy-to-do experiments, inventive arts and crafts
projects, fun games and puzzles, even science
biographies. From the earth and space sciences to
speculative fiction and ESP, this book will intrigue
every child with endless hours of science explo-
rations.

160 pp. $14.95 (0-673-16753-4)   Gr 3-6

Schoolyard Science

Children can explore and discover, measure
and chart, identify and name, collect and label,
and learn to do sci-
ence right outside
their school. There
are 25 terrific
hands-on science
experiments that
use easy-to-find
materials to teach
about weather, soil, plants, animals,
and even environmental issues.

96 pp. $8.95 (0-673-38967-7)   Gr 3-6

Diving Into Science

Here are 25 hands-on experiments for such
water-related topics as oil spills, submarines,

beach erosion,
and hermit crabs.
Experiments use
easily found mate-
rials and a discov-
ery approach to
guarantee success
and excitement.

Super Scientist activities integrate science with other subjects.

96 pp. $7.95 (0-673-38965-0)   Gr 3-6

Children's Literature

For literature-based science experiences, try these *Let's Read and Find Out Science Collection* sets. Each set includes a free teaching guide.

Set #1

Comets	Franklyn M. Branley
Is There Life in Outer Space?	Franklyn M. Branley
Journey Into a Black Hole	Franklyn M. Branley
The Moon Seems to Change	Franklyn M. Branley
The Planets in Our Solar System	Franklyn M. Branley
Rockets and Satellites	Franklyn M. Branley
The Sky Is Full of Stars	Franklyn M. Branley
What the Moon Is Like	Franklyn M. Branley

#063-70230-8   List price $36.00 (20% off) $28.80

Set #2

Air Is All Around You	Franklyn M. Branley
Flash, Crash, Rumble and Roll	Franklyn M. Branley
Gravity Is a Mystery	Franklyn M. Branley
Hurricane Watch	Franklyn M. Branley
Snow Is Falling	Franklyn M. Branley
Sunshine Makes the Seasons	Franklyn M. Branley
Volcanoes	Franklyn M. Branley
What Makes Day and Night	Franklyn M. Branley

#063-70231-6   List price $36.00 (20% off) $28.80

Set #3

Digging Up Dinosaurs	Aliki
Dinosaurs Are Different	Aliki
Fossils Tell of Long Ago	Aliki
Germs Make Me Sick!	Melvin Berger
My Five Senses	Aliki
My Visit to the Dinosaurs	Aliki
Rock Collecting	Roma Gans
What Happens to a Hamburger	Paul Showers
Wild and Woolly Mammoths	Aliki

#063-70232-4   List price $40.50   (20% off) $32.40

Scope and Sequence

activity	page	tool	module	skill	time needed	difficulty
1 Daytime/Nighttime	5	thermal card	introductory	making and using models	20-30 min.	easy
2 Where Are You Going?	7	magnet	introductory	inferring	20-30 min.	average
3 Make a Balloon Jet!	9	stopwatch	introductory	recognizing space relationships	15-20 min.	average
4 Life in a Drop	11	Fresnel lens	introductory	classifying	1 week	challenging
5 Quakes and Shakes	13	reflective paper	introductory	collecting and analyzing data	40-50 min.	challenging
6 The Color Spectrum	15	diffraction grating	introductory	classifying	30-40 min.	average
7 The Floating Ball	17	stopwatch	Module D	experimenting	15-20 min.	average
8 Salty Solutions	19	Fresnel lens	Module B	observing	2 weeks	challenging
9 Model Making	21	none	Module C	making and using models	15-20 min.	easy
10 Cool It!	23	stopwatch	Module E	predicting	20-30 min.	average
11 Pop Your Top!	25	none	Module C	inferring	30-40 min.	challenging
12 Bouncing Beams	27	reflective paper	Module F/C	experimenting	20-30 min.	average
13 Cool Cards	29	thermal card	Module D	predicting	30-40 min.	average
14 Free Fall	31	stopwatch	Module D	identifying and controlling variables	20-30 min.	challenging
15 Underwater Surprises	33	none	Module A	communicating	15-20 min.	easy
16 Planets—Hot and Cold	35	thermal card	Module A	interpreting data	40-50 min.	challenging
17 Lens Laboratory	37	Fresnel lens	Module A	making and using models	40-50 min.	challenging
18 Temperatures High and Low!	39	thermal card	Module E	measuring	40-50 min.	challenging
19 Hot and Cold	41	thermal card	Module E	predicting	2 weeks	challenging
20 Make It Sink!	43	stopwatch	Module B	recognizing time and space	30-40 min.	average
21 Looking at Light	45	diffraction grating	Module F	observing	20-30 min.	challenging
22 Magnet Mix-up	47	magnet	Module F	classifying	15-20 min.	easy
23 Storm Warnings	49	stopwatch	Module E	predicting	1 hour	challenging
24 Which Way Is the Wind Blowing?	51	none	Module E	experimenting	2 hours	challenging
25 Water Saver	53	stopwatch	Module B	measuring	2 hours	challenging
26 Matter in Motion	55	none	Module A	making a hypothesis	30-40 min.	average
27 Sound Speed	57	stopwatch	Module D	inferring	40-50 min.	challenging
28 Shake It, Don't Break It!	59	none	Module C	predicting	20-30 min.	average
29 Light Benders	61	reflective paper	Module F	experimenting	30-40 min.	average
30 Keep Warm! Stay Cool!	63	thermal card	Module E	inferring	40-50 min.	challenging

From the *ExploraCenter Activity Booklet.* Copyright © 1993 Scott, Foresman and Company.

Materials List

The following is a comprensive list of materials you will need to supplement the ExploraCenter in your classroom. These are all inexpensive and easy to find (see Resources that follow).

pencils
rubber bands
masking tape
graph paper
compass
iron nails
long narrow balloons
chairs
plastic drinking straws
meter sticks
string
small jars
glass dish
leaves
pond or rain water
grass
index cards
clay
flashlights
tables
white and black paper
colored paper
light sources
scissors
Ping Pong balls
hair dryer
chalk
cover goggles
water
table salt
drinking glasses
measuring spoons
overhead projector
plastic bowls

sealable bags
plastic film containers
white vinegar
baking powder
chalk erasers
ice cubes
heat sources
coffee filters
buckets
long rubber gloves
desk lamps
aquarium
cardboard
thermometer
aquarium gravel and sand
clear plastic bottles
food coloring
colored pencils
crayons
pennies
foil pie plate
soda cans
paper clips
paper plates
pins
glue
8 ounce paper cups
water fountain
Ivory™ liquid soap
drums
drumsticks
paper towels
dessert gelatin
desks
sunny window

To buy additional ExploraCenter tool kits, please call ScottForesman at 1-800-554-4411.

From the *ExploraCenter Activity Booklet.* Copyright © 1993 Scott, Foresman and Company.